LIBERATION
IN
MIDDLE AMERICA

LIBERATION
IN
MIDDLE AMERICA

Gabriel Fackre

A Pilgrim Press Book
Philadelphia

Library of Congress
Catalog Card Number 74-178752

ISBN 0-8298-0225-8

CONTENTS

To longtime friends and "mid-libs"—

Frank and Gertrude Pirazzini

Jerry and Elisabeth Jud

George and Danny Geisler

Herb and Lillian Davis

Like some of the "visionary realists" mentioned in this volume, the author has come through the struggles of the sixties for racial justice and peace with his dreams of a human world still intact. But like them also, he has a much more sober appreciation of the ambiguities to be found among both "the children of light and the children of darkness," and a clearer understanding of the social power required to lend reality to the finest of visions. Although we must transpose the somber notes of yesterday's Christian realism into a more hopeful key, as I have tried to show in *The Promise of Reinhold Niebuhr*,[1] we are not done with the searching observations on human pretension by that giant among theologians and social thinkers. Such a neorealism, grounded in Niebuhr but stretched by the futurists and visionaries with whom I have worked over the past decade, has led me into this exploration of middle America. Behind the pejoratives are people. And with them is power.

The inquiry has gone on apace in three rather different middle American locales: the small city of Lancaster, Pennsylvania, from which the two models are drawn; Honolulu, Hawaii, where, during a leave of absence, I had a chance to test some of the theses at the creative Church of the Crossroads; and in suburban Boston where an NIP (*Newton Independent Press*) is being born after the fashion of chapter 8's LIP. Back of this white-collar life lie ten years in a Pittsburgh steel town, upon which the book's working-class reflections draw heavily.

Why should someone who is a theologian by trade write a book like this? There are two answers. One is that faith's visions of liberation and reconciliation and its perception of the realities of sin and finitude propel it into an arena where both hopes and hurts are much in evidence. But there is a very pedestrian reason as well. The church is right in the middle of middle America. It is our "turf." This community of memory and hope could make a difference if it had a good feel of the terrain and knew where it wanted to go. The book aims to supply a few charts for the faith company, as well as a compass or two for a wider constituency.

The author is grateful to Gladys Lambert at Lancaster Theological Seminary and Dolores Kronberg at Andover Newton Theological School, whose expertise went into the production of the manuscript.

For much light shed on this subject I am indebted to my favorite middle American (liberated), my wife. Her banners flew over LIP's office, her pop design buttons kept the paper solvent at critical junctures, and her photographs livened its early issues. She also chaired PACE at its inception and got up in the middle of the night to answer the anonymous phone calls that breathed their fury upon us. One of the words Dot coined for her buttons and banners is a good note to sound for the liberation hopes of the seventies—"aiglatson"—forward nostalgia, an appetite whetted for the future.

ACKNOWLEDGMENTS

I appreciate the cooperation of various publishers in allowing me to reprint material from previous essays of mine: an earlier version of chapter 5 appeared as an article in *The Christian Century* 86, no. 19 (May 7, 1969). Copyright 1969 Christian Century Foundation. Reprinted by permission. An earlier version of chapter 7 titled "Going East: Neomysticism and Christian Faith" appeared in *The Christian Century* 85, no. 15 (April 14, 1971). Copyright 1971 Christian Century Foundation. Reprinted by permission. An earlier version of chapter 8 was published in *Journal* 7, no. 11 (September 1969), published by the Division of Higher Education, United Church Board for Homeland Ministries. An earlier version of chapter 9 was part of the author's monograph *Second Fronts in Metropolitan Mission* (Grand Rapids: W. D. Eerdmans Company, 1968). Used by permission.

PART I

THE HURTS AND HOPES
OF THE SILENT MAJORITY

Who are the middle Americans? What are their anguishes and expectations? In the first section we explore the new interest in blue- and white-collar citizenry. Behind it is the phenomenon of dehumanization pinpointed by an earlier literature of alienation and current critique of technocracy. And ahead of it lie some visions of liberation and hope.

Chapter 1
THE BLUE-GREENING
OF AMERICA

"The ignored man of the sixties is the star of the seventies," writes Louise Howe in *The White Majority*.[1] The fairly recent discovery of both the alienation and the power of blue- and white-collar communities has been less the achievement of artistic and literary barometers of social change and more the result of pulse-taking media people like Mrs. Howe. Philadelphia newsman Peter Binzen explores the anger of ethnic citizens in *Whitetown, USA*; Richard Lemon puts together extensive *Newsweek* data in *The Troubled American*; Marshall Frady monitors the anger of workers in *Harper's Magazine* and in his brilliant study *Wallace*; *Time-Life's* and later *New Republic's* Alexander Campbell describes the aches and pains of the silent majority in *The Trouble with Americans*; Studs Terkel examines Depression-drenched memories in *Hard Times*; Scammon and Wattenberg join journalistic talent and census-tract data to produce an election year handbook on *The Real Majority*. Not to be outdone, the film-maker and the TV writer favor us with frightening portraits of hardhats "Joe" and Archie Bunker, and confrontations on the shop floor between "good grammar and good taste."

Together with the popular pointers to forgotten America, there has been the more recent scholarly research and think-tank inquiry probing the psyche and social patterns of the blue collar-white collar world. Herman Kahn's Hudson Institute has spent considerable time ferreting out the mood of middle America, particularly in the studies under the aegis of Frank Armbruster.[2] Andrew Greeley at the National Opinion Research Center has reported his research in *Why Can't They Be Like Us?* Arthur Shostak produced an important study in *Blue-Collar Life*. Bensman and Vidich have done their usual competent job in *The New American Society: The Revolution of the Middle Class*. Among the early efforts at reassessing the role of ethnic groups was that of the American Jewish Committee in its survey *The Reacting Americans*. Perhaps the first to ring the bell directing attention to ethnic communities were Daniel Moynihan and Nathan Glazer in their recently republished and rediscovered *Beyond the Melting Pot.* Very early pioneers in sociological overview of both wings of the phenomenon we deal with here are Mirra Komarovsky's *Blue-Collar Marriage* and C. Wright Mills's *White Collar.*

Leadership in the political arena has made active use of some of these soundings, particularly those politicians whose own roots and constituencies are middle American: Greek-American Spiro Agnew, Polish-American Edmund Muskie, "Southern-American" George Wallace. While some of the rhetoric attempts to give voice to the agonies of the silent center in concert with other harassed citizens—minority groups, for example—more often manipulation and irritation of middle American anger is the order of the day.

Visionary Realism

There is, however, another breed of "politician" who is trying to raise the hopes rather than exploit the hurts of middle America. Sam Brown, one of the organizers of the November 1969 Vietnam Moratorium, embodies this new style and expresses its perspective in these remarks:

> The middle-income worker who finds himself unable to afford a lawyer or the increase in his health insurance policy is in many ways like the student who cannot get a straight answer from his government about a ridiculously immoral war. It is not simply the inability to change policy, it is the inability to even determine what the policy is, or who has the power to change it once it is determined.
> The most pressing contemporary political challenge is to begin building a coalition of the underrepresented, a coalition of the small, aimed at letting some of the air out of the professional guilds and government bureaucracies and controlling the corporate concentrations which exercise vast public power behind a mask of private competition.[3]

Saul Alinsky has sent out a call for such a coalition in his recent *Rules for Radicals* and plans to devote his time increasingly to the organizing of middle Americans for the struggle to democratize corporate power. Monsignor Geno Baroni, fresh from Selma and other struggles for black justice, now focuses on the dehumanization of blue-collar communities and seeks to generate "ethnic power" that will deal with working-class grievances. Ralph Nader, without self-conscious identity tags, is in fact a spokesman for a middle American constituency whose vulnerability is bound up with the consumption patterns to which it has tied itself. It is these kinds of new change agents that will set the pace for social transformation in the next decade. Incidentally, an interesting fact about both the activists and the scholarly and popular researchers is their own ethnic roots. One of the realities about social change is that it is proximity and sensitivity to the plight of their own people that produce change agents. And this is as it should be, even as black scholarship and leadership have sounded and will continue to sound the alarm for the anguish of its own people.

A crucial mark of style and strategy, developed in many cases out of the struggles in the sixties in the movements for black justice, peace, and the rights of the poor, is the "visionary realism" of the ethnic activist. Let's look at two dimensions of that identity.

Visionary realists learned to dream the dreams of Martin Luther King, Jr. They are part of a new consciousness in our society, not limited to but usually including the "greening" young of the sixties, that is profoundly sensitive to the neighbor's need, a neighbor that includes all the victims of poverty and injustice on the modern Jericho roads. The singularity of their own vision is its inclusion among the wounded of those that the conventional rhetoric of the Left consigned to hell—"hardhats," "greasers," "rednecks," "pigs," and suburbanites. While they are fully aware that the depth of the blue- and white-collar wounds cannot be compared to those of a starving Pakistani or the rat bites and hopeless future of a ghetto child, they also know that the same kind of economic and social futility plagues the lives of middling millions in an affluent America.

Further, they understand in non-Marxist terms a fundamental Marxist assumption: poverty is relative to the resources and expectations of a given society. It is precisely those who are led to believe there are ways to make life livable—and that they themselves have been graced with that opportunity—who are most conscious of the disparity between promise and performance, and most pained and angry about this breach. We now begin to perceive the poison in the air, the water, and the soil upon

14

which we depend for survival, and the cancerous taints in the processed food upon which we depend for nourishment. We become aware of the uncertainties, exorbitant cost, and depersonalization of much of our medical and dental care; the unnerving and dangerous traffic warfare in which we daily engage in suicidally unsafe cars (while 45,000 of our countrymen were dying in Indochinese warfare since 1959, 500,000 of us were being destroyed in the vehicular confrontations in our streets); the decrepit and demeaning public transportation inflicted upon urban commuters; the regimented and dehumanizing state of our children's public education that is finally being held up to the light of public exposure; the job insecurities that hang alike over the Pittsburgh steelworker and the Boston Route 128 engineer; the "crudity" of life in the cities and nearby suburbs—from filth, noise, and physical danger to the breakdown of utility services to the lethargy and corruption of our leaders; the plight of the aged, who are house prisoners in the winter because there is no sidewalk snow policy and captives in the summer because there are no streetlights or police to protect them from assault; the ticky-tackiness of the products we buy, from toys for the children to the houses we live in; the growing fears of surveillance over our lives by government that can even anger the most middle American of congressmen; and, topping it all off, the cruel and inane war that takes its heaviest numerical toll on the children of middle America and consumes billions in funds that could be put to work to heal the social sores here catalogued.

As painful as these physical hurts are, there are other wounds that fell white middle Americans the same as the poor, the black, the brown, and the red. Sensitivity to these debilities is part of the equipment of visionaries who perceive what a human society could be and is not. Dehumanization, as we shall try to show in chapter 2, is just as much a destructive set of relationships as it is eroded goods and services. And preeminently that means powerlessness. Middle Americans feel that their lives are controlled by decisions made in distant Kafka-like castles. They are right. Part of the sickness of our technocratic society is the incapacity of the VLP's (Very Little Persons) to exercise any significant influence over the VIP's, who by acts of commission or omission chart and sail our social course. Humanization means, therefore, the empowerment of the citizenry and the repossession from technocratic elites and structures of the control over our future. The young, the black, and the poor are "getting it together." And the middle American is about to join them.

Visionaries not only have a picture in their heads of a humane society, and a sharp awareness of our current killing of that dream, but also a perception of a new factor: the rising consciousness of middle America. Perhaps that awareness stands along the boundary between vision and reality. There is not only a manifest hurt in middle America, but there is also a growing self-awareness of that gaping wound and a determination to do something about it. Early symptoms may take strange forms, as we shall presently note, but they suggest something deeper. The silent center hurts, and knows that it does. It now gives off signals that it plans to do something about it. Visionaries therefore do their dreaming in range of reality. There may be a pregnant moment in the seventies when the mighty shall tumble from their seats and there shall be "exalted . . . those of low degree."

How desperately visionaries are needed in a time when middle American bread is rising. Enablers are required who can bring together the forces of liberation in a common struggle. If that does not happen, the destructive polarities of the sixties—in which the minority dissenter was pitted against the silent majority—will continue and worsen. The technocracy that profited from this internecine struggle among potential allies will once again have succeeded in its diversionary tactics. The gift of vision is one that sees the full range of slaveries that cry for liberation and point toward coalitions of all the forgotten Americans. A visionary is a rainbow-maker who gathers together the blue and white with the black, the brown, and the red.

If there is just a pinch of realism in the visionary's perception that middle America's humanization is an idea whose time has come, then there is a fistful of it in his grasp of the nature of power and where it lies in our society. What makes him a visionary *realist* is simply put by Saul Alinsky: "Organization for action will now and in the decade ahead center upon America's white middle class. That is where the power is." [4] To pursue to

full term the near-aborted social developments of the 1960's—
the visions of liberation of the young, the black, and the poor—
there must be more facilitating energies than those movements
have been able to generate on their own. In the American context those energies have nothing to do with the artillery about
which adventurists fantasize. As Hannah Arendt argues, it is not
violence but power that is decisive in social change or social
continuity.[5] That kind of power in our setting lies in the numbers and ethos of middle America. If any of our visions of a
more humane society are to be fulfilled, they will have to catch
the eye of this sector of the population. That the troubled
American now is in the position to see the glint of that kind of
light—by virtue of his peering up out of the same morass as
other victims—gives some credibility to the hope that his power
can be harnessed to the engines of his fellow sufferer struggling
up out of "the Pit" (see chapter 6). Visionary realism, therefore,
is a kind of sober hope committed to dreaming dreams of liberation for all the faceless and nameless, and believing that such a
struggle has some chance of success if the powers of blue- and
white-collar communities are mated to those of other alienated
Americans.

Who Are the Middle Americans?

In popular usage the phrase middle America often characterizes
citizens holding a set of attitudes that opt for flag-waving instead of flag-burning, strong support for law and order, distaste
for "hippies" and "longhairs," resentment of "uppity niggers,"
and "welfare chiselers," and so on. If this were the case, a
wealthy Texas oilman or an aged black apologist for the John
Birch Society might qualify as middle American. But rather
than using the concept to identify a state of mind or system of
values, we employ it here as a description of Americans with a
particular economic and social location. Specifically, we borrow
the reference points used by Scammon and Wattenberg: the
"unyoung," the "unpoor," and the "unblack." [6]
    In addition to rooting itself more carefully in manageable em-
pirical data, our definition leaves maneuvering room for the thesis of this study: middle Americans can be liberated from their
captivity. That slavery includes not only the physical and socio-

logical debilities mentioned earlier, but also the ideology which both softens and hides those hurts. Thus we do not believe that "hardhats" are fated to pulverize "peaceniks," or suburban whites to fend off urban blacks. In fact, we view our inquiry as a manual calculated to overcome these disastrous polarities.

The Unyoung

Middle America is middle aged. We take here the counterculture's "over thirty" target as the lower age boundary of our subject population. But middle America is unold as well as unyoung. The subcultures of the aged and the retired, and the growing self-consciousness of "senior power," suggest a demarcation also at the upper level, somewhere around sixty years of age.

The Unpoor

Depending on the year when studies of middle America are made, the income range varies greatly. In the early seventies middle American annual income received from wages or salary would begin somewhere over the poverty line of an affluent, inflation-prone society at, let us say, about $5,000. Because middle America is unrich as well as unpoor, it would range upward to about $15,000.[7]

As to class, the spectrum runs from the semiskilled factory worker and store clerk, through secretaries, skilled workers, sales people, and civil servants, to merchants, technicians, teachers, and preachers. On Lloyd Warner's Index of Status Characteristics scale,[8] the range of citizenry would extend from UL (upper lower) through LM (lower middle) (with the clear presence of C. Wright Mills's earlier and Bensman and Vidich's later "new middle classes,"[9] and therefore a very strong component also of "middle middle"). Middle America is a blue-collar/white-collar mix.

The Unblack

While the word colored has, outside the British Commonwealth, been captured by racist and paternalist associations, Colin Morris's word uncolored is a more accurate description of the non-black, nonbrown, nonred, nonyellow middle American constituency. Middle America is the "white majority" about which Louise Howe speaks or, more exactly, the colorless shade that befits its general middling range. And it lives in its ghettos (more of its own choosing than the inner city imprisonments of the black or the reservations of the red, but for all that, discernible enclaves) : the small towns and small cities that dot the land, the working-class neighborhoods of metropolis, and the inner rings of suburbia.

Middle America, therefore, is an adjective that points to a middling breed of humanity, between the extremes of poverty and affluence, young and old, inner city and exurbia, lacking even any sharp color differential. There are from seventy to eighty million such centrists in our midst, depending on the surveyor. Pallid though they be, middle Americans hold the real political power in this country (Scammon and Wattenberg), or at least the swing position in social change. They are also human beings with names and faces, hopes and hurts. Probably "they" should read "we," for it is more than likely that the reader as well as the writer of this book are to be numbered among the unyoung, unpoor, and the unblack.

Religion and Middle America

An interesting presence in middle American commentary and action makes itself evident in some of the protagonists earlier cited, such as Geno Baroni and Andrew Greeley, and such institutions as the American Jewish Committee. To these could be added Michael Novak, Peter Berger, Peter Riga, the Committee of Southern Churchmen and its magazine *Katallegete,* the Detroit Industrial Mission, and such widely read journals of the Catholic, Jewish, and Protestant communities as *Commonweal, Commentary,* and *The Christian Century.* Could it be that just as Martin Luther King, Jr., and Coretta King, Jessie Jackson, Andrew Young, and countless other black churchmen gave forceful expression to the grievances of their own constituencies, so too middle America will find its voice through some of its religious institutions and leaders? The renegade Baptist chaplain praying over the Ku Klux Klan rally was an early and demonic megaphone of the alienated southern white. Billy Graham, shamefully accrediting the Nixon exploitation of middle American fears, is a later and more sophisticated version of the same bastardized religious reaction.

It appears that a different kind of religious response is in the making, one that shares the anguish of middle America but at the same time takes sharp issue with its prejudices and animosities. Whether this critical alliance and dialetical companionship, prepared to say both yes and no to middle American ferment, has a future in the seventies is too early to predict. In any case, the scenarios being spun out by the Baronis and Bergers will be factors to be reckoned with in the next decade.

This book and the experiments in liberation it describes rise out of the author's religious commitments and background in middle America. As a second-generation half-Arab raised in a Brooklyn working-class neighborhood, and attending a high school with large Jewish and black constituencies, one soon learns hard facts about both the need for and difficulty of the kind of intra- and inter-middle American alliances here pled for. Two years at a mission church in Mayor Daley's own neighborhood, the Bridgeport section of Chicago, and a ten-year ministry with Pittsburgh workers in the steel towns of Homestead and Duquesne brought me very close to the "Turkey Sams" and "Mabels" described in part II. Another decade in the Pennsylvania Dutch heartland of middle America prompted the exploration of the kinds of models sketched in part IV. In addition to the synoptic views and strategies attempted in this work, I have done some piecemeal reflection on mill-town issues and more basic research in the nature of modern alienation.[10]

Out of this journey through middle America has come for me a deep affection for the working-class men and women so damningly caricatured in the Joes and Archie Bunkers of the film and television world. And white-collar clerks and Route 128 technicians are human too. Whether one views that humanity through the haze that hangs over the battles of the sixties, during which our subjects seem to be on the other side of the barricades, remains to be seen. In any case, the moral commitments and massive institutional presence of the faith community in middle America give it a special mandate to work for the day when John Doe gets back his name and his face.

The Blue-greening of America

In *The Greening of America* Charles Reich contends that there are new forces at work among the young that are on the way to humanizing our technocratic world. A counterculture vanguard, with the beads and bellbottoms of its Consciousness III, will gently erode the old ways of both small-town society and the corporate state. Surely something is afoot. But the greening of America is taking place on a wider scale and goes deeper than the turning of upper-middle-class youth.

In a perceptive critique of the Reich thesis Brigitte and Peter Berger speak about the "blueing of America." [11] Among other things they refer to the occupation by the sons and daughters of middle America of that terrain heretofore the possession of the affluent and elite. The leadership vacuum, left by the opting out of large numbers of children of privilege on the pilgrimage to the greener pastures of the communes or colonies of more satisfying life-style, is being filled by upwardly mobile middle American young. This development lends further weight to the argument here that middle America holds a key position in the social struggles of the seventies.

However, we want to put the Reich and Berger theses together in a new gestalt. Blue-collar America is itself undergoing a process of greening. Involved is not merely the changing hair and life-styles beginning to manifest themselves in working-class communities, although these stigmata are clues. There is a growing alienation of blue-collar young and old from the technocratic systems that dehumanize their lives as much as they estrange the young of the upper middle class. And in tandem with this, here and there the first shoots of the blue-green grass of liberation can be seen coming up through the asphalt of the mill town.

We want to stretch the color spectrum further than its Reichian limits. And beyond the blue as well, to the blue-white. We find the liberated middle American in the ranks of the white-collar citizenry suffering from the debilities that now lace all sectors of society. Loosened up by powerful cultural forces, drawn by new vision, *The Radical Suburb,* as John Orr and F. Patrick Nelson call it,[12] is now a factor to be taken much into account. While we are widening the boundaries of modern ferment in peace and freedom, let it be traced also to its pioneering color: black. It was in the dreams of Martin Luther King, Jr., and those who struggled alongside him for black justice that the visions of a human world were most powerfully generated in our recent past. And now the brown, the tan, and the red join that stride toward freedom. When all is said and done, it is really the "rainbowing of America" that is taking place.

The river is deeper and wider than the soundings of Reich have suggested. The dimension of depth here is intended to describe some of the motive forces at work in the movements for liberation. Romantics may view the soft visionaries of the counterculture, or the hard visionaries of revolution, as moved by compassion and goodwill. A more sober assessment of the motives of social change detects also factors of survival and self-interest. The personal dangers and inconveniences of military service, as well as the love of mankind, swell the ranks of the peace movement. Anger at the boredom and futility of much pedagogy, as well as idealistic reform of higher education, has contributed to the campus surges of the sixties. Blue-collar and white-collar militancy about the recreational environment is no accident when you add up how many workers hunt and fish and how many lower-middle-class family campers and trailers are on the summer roads.

Middle Americans are joining the consumer revolution too, as they awaken to the deterioration and dangers of their food, goods, and services. Those most vulnerable to social wounds, the poor and the black, cannot wait upon the luxury of somebody else's idealism to propel them out of their abyss, so they muster whatever power they can around their own survival and advancement impulses. And why not? The will to survive and live a human life has to be harnessed to social goals if change is to be effective, even while the transmuting of that instinct into a will to power over others must be resisted. That is the visionary realism of which we have spoken. And it is the confluence of realism and vision that makes the blue-green stream a powerful one.

Paul Tillich said that the difference between wishful thinking and hope is evidence. Because we have the hard data of new life and movement in our time in the blue-greening process, there is hope. The somber forecasts of intractable polarization and the fearful comparisons between Germany of the thirties and America of the seventies become less credible as the varied expressions of liberation assert themselves.

But as hope is not fantasy, neither is it error-free forecast. Liberation is possible, but not certain. And in middle America, with its variety and ambiguity, even the most sophisticated Delphic projection is murky at best. So here we nurse, for the foreseeable future, modest hopes: not yet a full-scale liberation of, but rather liberation *in*, middle America. And we look for and work for those firstfruits of a human tomorrow among those members of the silent majority that have found their voice.

Chapter 2

DEHUMANIZATION
IN MIDDLE AMERICA

Erich Fromm observed in 1955 in his *Sane Society* that the problem of the nineteenth century was "God is dead," and the problem of the twentieth century is "Man is dead." "Dehumanization" was a theme that threaded its way through much of the social, cultural, literary, and religious commentary of the World War II and postwar periods. It is manifest in the spectrum of philosophical existentialism from Sartre to Marcel. It appears in the cultural critics: the "alienation" accents of Fromm, Herbert Marcuse, and C. Wright Mills, Dwight MacDonald's bewailment of kitsch, David Riesman's "lonely crowd," Vance Packard's "hidden persuaders," and William Whyte's "organization man." Poets and novelists from T. S. Eliot to the Beats spin requiems for "hollow men" and "fables for the final hour." And dehumanization plays a prominent role in the thinking of such religious interpreters as Martin Buber, Paul Tillich, Jacques Maritain, Nicholas Berdyaev, Emil Brunner, and even Karl Barth.

In retrospect it is striking to note that much of this commentary had to do with the frustrations and degradations of middle America, or their equivalent in other societies. Not all of them, of course. The heaviest burden of dehumanization fell upon the poor, the black, and the young. Like the latter who began to marshal their forces in the sixties to fight back, it is likely that the struggle for rehumanization will widen to include middle Americans. In order to gain perspective on the total phenomenon and its direction, it is helpful to study the early warning signals in the literature of alienation.

Dimensions of Dehumanization

The ingenuity and spread of the terminology used in characterizing the loss of human reality is impressive: depersonalization, thingification, alienation, robotization, automatization, maceration, abstractification, quantification, regimentation, insectification, homogenization, segmentalization, standardization, disintegration, calculation, manipulation, expropriation; nihilism, estrangement, other-directedness, groupiness, conformism; mass man, organization man, functionary, spectator, cog in machine; making men into objects, making men into means, and the classic Buberian I-It orientation. Analysts of this phenomenon deal with a variety of relationships, attitudes, and institutions which are believed to be the source of the problem. We attempt here to devise a typology that sorts out the categories of criticism.[1]

Utility
Versus Affirmation-Union

Things are for use and people are for love. When people are used and things are loved, something has gone amiss. Much dehumanization critique can be summed up in this formula, with a stress upon the use theme. Under attack here is the image of man as an object of utility. Protest is made against viewing man as a "commodity" or "means for economic profit" (Fromm,[2] Tillich [3]) or as "material" for disposal by an authoritarian state of the Left or the Right (Gollwitzer,[4] Thielicke,[5] Koestler [6]), as an object of self-manipulation in the personality market (Mills [7]), or as a sex object (Harvey Cox writing about *Playboy* magazine[8]). Instead of the self being unconditionally affirmed in the relationship, the self is viewed as a thing to be used, disused, or abused. I exist *for* another instead of being in union with that other. Thus the dehumanized self can become a vote in a politician's pocket, the dues card on the union roster, the cog in the factory machine, and so on.

Abstractification Versus
Full-orbed Concrete Relation

Very closely bound up with utility-dehumanization, yet distinguishable from it, is abstractification.[9] Here the relation of the other to the self is controlled by a truncated image. Rich, full human concreteness is erased as one strand of the self's being is plucked out and held up as definitive. The hospital system that conceives of John Jenkins as "the ulcer in 304," [10] the company that views its workers as "hands," the newspaper that treats the accident victim as "news," the racist who disdains "the colored" all represent a reductionism that substitutes an abstraction for concrete reality.

True, Jenkins has an ulcer and his room number is 304, workers do have hands, the accident is news, the child making her way to the integrated school is black. Dehumanization happens when the *hasness* of these adjectival facts is transformed into *isness,* when a partial relation becomes a controlling and definitive one.

Martin Buber says that men are fated to become "its" for other men in that the "experience" of others is a necessary phase of living.[11] We cannot constantly breathe the rarified air of the I-Thou meeting; we must descend periodically to the lower plane of relating to others as if they were numbers, things, objects. While this melancholy observation does recognize the impossibility of maintaining the purity of communion in our finite world, and also reminds us of the dehumanizing dangers in abstractification, it tends to obscure the rehumanizing possibilities of I-It relationships themselves. The doctor focusing a cold diagnostic light on the ulcer for the purposes of healing, the Social Security check that pays the rent, the telephone number available in time of emergency are all crucial ways of affirming the Thouness of human beings. Nevertheless, the statistical tendencies of mass society surely lend themselves to the dangers of human erosion, especially when having a number fades into being a number.

The Impersonal Versus the Intimate

Sheer size comes in for its share of criticism in dehumanization thinking. Big government, big industry, big unions, big cities are seen to be alienating forces in their estrangement of leadership from the grass roots, their destruction of primary relations, and their impediments to participatory life. Rehumanization in the face of vast impersonalness is sought regularly through the recovery of the small unit. This theme appears in the communitarian programs of Buber [12] and Fromm,[13] Whyte's desire to restore or protect the personal and familiar in urban living,[14] Lewis Mumford's and Robert Nisbet's proposals to reduce large social units to manageable proportions.[15]

Entering this debate are those who maintain that bigness as such is not evil. David Lilienthal points out that size has contributed greatly to American productivity and efficiency.[16] Will Herberg asserts that communitarian forms relevant to other cultures do not have a legitimate place in large-scale American society and that there are dangerous seeds of "totalism" in such endeavors.[17]

Under the first three rubrics we have dealt with relationships in which human beings find themselves. In the final three categories we examine the effects on humans of those relationships.

Inhumanity

The inhuman treatment of human beings refers here to physical deprivation and its radical form, destruction of life. Much critiquing of dehumanization assumes that the factory barbarities and pauperization associated with the burgeoning industrialism of the eighteenth and nineteenth centuries have given way to subtler forms of human defacement. But Michael Harrington and others are on hand to uncover the miseries of tens of millions in "the other America." [18]

Inhumanity is, however, very much a part of dehumanization critique when totalitarianism is under the glass. The horrendous extermination programs of the Nazis and the liquidation policies in Stalinist Russia are pointed to as inhuman results of the dehumanizing images of persons as objects of utility or disutility. And the ominous possibilities of a nuclear age, in which military minds ponder such risks as "We might lose fifty million but the other side will lose one hundred million," are seen in all their inhuman horror.

The Stunting
of "the Higher Faculties"

Critics have turned their microscopes on the contemporary smothering of men's intellectual, aesthetic, and spiritual potentialities. Here the target is often the manipulation of mass man. Various aspects of this kind of dehumanization have been portrayed: the cheapening effect on the psyche of the fantasy world of TV (Newton Minow, David Susskind, John Crosby and the

scholarly studies *Mass Culture* and *Mass Leisure* [19]), the erosion
of sensibilities by advertising, and kitsch in all its forms (Packard,[20] Meerloo,[21] Rosenberg [22]), and the anti-intellectualism of
political and religious demagoguery are all familiar strokes in
this picture.

The Denial of Self-determination

Here there is a wide spectrum of protest. It ranges from the students of the early Marx (Marcuse [23] and Fromm [24]), who dwell
upon social and self-alienation, through the general attack on
the totalitarian state, to the critics of profit-oriented mass
media, the proponents of industrial democracy through union
initiative (Golden and Rutenberg[25]) or worker participation
in decision-making (John XXIII[26]) or on-the-job recognition
(Mayo [27]), and the insistence on worker self-determination
within the union (Lens [28]). Setting the stage for revolutions
soon to be born were the cries for black justice by Martin Luther King, Jr.,[29] and the student charter of freedom embodied
in the Port Huron Statement.[30] Common to all is the declaration of men's right to shape their own destiny independent of
the "principalities and powers" that hover above them.

Technocracy

Since the early period of dehumanization criticism, our society
has experienced shock waves of anger among many of those
treated as objects of manipulation and contempt. The protest
movements of the blacks, Puerto Ricans, Chicanos, American Indians, students, welfare mothers, consumers, and women not
only began to make visible the human being behind the statistics, but also exposed more clearly the sources of alienation. And
an accelerating technology harnessed to the engines of a cruel
and unpopular war, together with its increasing devastation of
the natural environment, further revealed the scabs on the
whore of our modern Babylon. Out of this maelstrom a new
chapter in social commentary is being born, one which extends
and refines the earlier interpretations of dehumanization. In literature that runs from Theodore Roszak's *The Making of a
Counter Culture* [31] to Alvin Toffler's *Future Shock* [32] it is

technocracy that appears as the systemic blight on our culture. In its institutions, processes, and commitments are to be found the mechanisms of dehumanization. Let us attempt to identify the components of technocracy:

1. The belief that the methods and momentum of scientific technology can and will create a viable society.

2. "Econocentrism" (Toffler) —a confident faith in economic growth as the polestar of that society.

3. Present-orientation—the focus upon, and drive toward, immediate achievements and satisfactions with little or no attention to either the short- or long-range social consequences or environmental effects of Now-focused technological and econocentric activity.

4. The location of political, social, and economic power in vast corporate entities with no effective system of checks and balances.

5. Decision-making vested in corporate elites: on the one hand, managerial generalists, and on the other, highly specialized technicians, with no responsible methods of accountability to those affected by their decisions.

It is this technocratic juggernaut that is rolled over the helpless in man and nature. As the agent of dehumanizing relationships and effects, its victims include the young, the poor, the women, the black, brown, and red, the blue-collar and white-collar masses, and the air, water, and soil on which they depend for life and breath. All six dimensions of dehumanization manifest themselves in the tribulations of a technocratic society, but two in particular lurch to center stage: inhumanity and the sense of loss of self-determination.

Both the level of inhumanity and our perception of it have escalated since the postwar studies of alienation. The war years that have taken such a heavy toll on a generation of Indochinese have raised up a growing army of fellow sufferers in the American under class and middle class. Along with this is continuing poverty and despair in the urban ghettos and forgotten rural slums. And joined to deprivation is a new degradation of the quality of life which is apparent to the most superficial observer of the state of garbage collection, street repair, public transportation, schools, housing, hospitals, mental institutions, medical and dental services, homes for the aged, traffic, consumer goods, social services, electric power, water supply, prisons, courts, air, and food. Alexander Campbell's somber catalogue of the miseries we conceal by our myths is well worth pondering.[33]

Behind the daily dangers is the sense of powerlessness. It expresses itself in a paradoxical way: on one hand, a conviction that the future is in the hands of manipulating power structures and, on the other, the fear that we drift along from crisis to crisis because "nobody is in charge." Both the elitism and the economic immediacy-orientation of technocracy give substance to these perceptions.

Technocracy's steamroller has produced responses that run from the bizarre to the explosive. Chemical fantasy and neomystical reverie in the counterculture of the young represent both protest against, and flight from, the rational empirical techniques whose fruits seem to be the hardware of war and blight. The quest for community, ruptured by the mechanisms and individualisms of technocracy, leads to the utopian commune or the togetherness of an encounter group. The ritual "flaggery" and superpatriotism of middle America are themselves distress signals of dehumanization. And for the lowest levels of the under class whose lives have been most seriously wounded there is always heroin, hooch, and holy rolling. Alongside these symptoms of anguish there is more aggressive feedback: the clenched fist and the midnight bomb of the terrorist.

While the exotic and erratic careened through the sixties, another more powerful and lasting force was asserting itself. The central thrusts for liberation of the black, the young, and the poor made their presence felt by their large constituencies and determined assaults on the strongholds of alienation. Black citizens marched and organized for public accommodations, access to the polls and government, justice in jobs, housing, and education. The young challenged the educational autocracies and the war machine that sought to devour them. The poor took on their landlords and welfare bureaucracies. It was becoming clear that some segments of the population would no longer tolerate their treatment as manipulable things in a degraded environment. Further, the powerless sought empowerment in their struggle to regain their humanity: black power, student power, poor power.

What of the unblack, the unyoung, and the unpoor? The many labor-union placards and the large church contingent in the 1963 Washington March were small signs of an early affirmation of this new surge by slices of middle America. But as minority pressure built, this tentative alliance began to shred. A variety of factors were at work. The economic and geographic proximity of blue- and white-collar America to the liberation breakouts of minority groups meant that middle America was the first to experience the effects of rapid social change. Because the "size of the pie" did not seem to expand in proportion to the number of new pieces being cut, minorities and middle Americans had to battle one another for the crumbs to improve crowded urban education, neighborhoods, and economic opportunities. On top of that came exposure to a whole range of new sights, sounds, smells, and life-styles from the cultures of the young, as well as the black and the poor—and middle America had neither the preparation nor the resources in its own set of commitments to cope with them. And suffering from the same egocentricities and envies to which all collectivities are prone, we middle Americans tended to resent both the surge forward of protesters and the attention they commanded in the media. We became an angry "silent majority" of "forgotten Americans."

Meanwhile, the structures and structurers of technocracy responsible for the hunger of minority groups, and the small and stale pie being wrestled over by middle and under classes, remained above the battle and largely unaddressed. Its spokesmen in the political forum actively exploited the fears of middle Americans, encouraging vicious stereotypes and characterizing liberation efforts as the work of drug-drenched hippies, cowardly draft-dodgers and traitors, riotous and libertine longhairs, crime-plotting blacks, and welfare chiselers, all bent upon destroying God, mother, and country. This clever diversionary tactic blinded the contenders to the fact of their shared plight and common foe, and made impossible any united attack on the dehumanizing forces set in motion by the technocracy.

The final irony came with the accrediting of the technocratic myth by some of the loudest spokesmen of the New Left. We were told that society was splitting into two camps: in the one were the visionary young, the doves, the swingers, the militant blacks, and the wretched of the earth; in the other, were the over thirties, the squares, the hawks, the hardhats, the pigs, the uptight whites, and the fat cats of suburbia. The conventional wisdom of "the forces of revolution" simply succeeded in driving a further wedge between potential allies, thus denying to minority groups the social power that might have given the coup de grace to the sources of their own estrangement.[34]

The notorious Boston area traffic war suggests itself as a picture of the congeries of forces at work in the dehumanization of the sixties. Driver is pitted against driver, driver against pedestrian and cyclist, and cyclist and pedestrian against driver. Tempers mount, the timid become demonic, acts of rudeness and hostility unthinkable in normal social intercourse become daily fare. Why? While there is the rhetoric of safety and humanity, there are no rules, or those charged with enforcing them do not do so, or the rules are so inane as to invite violation. Thus a green light beckons two lines of cars to fight their way across a street into one lane, while a red light across from a police station means no more than "Look before you leap," if that, to a savvy driver. Nicely painted crosswalks hurl pedestrians into impassable maelstroms, while neither a centered line nor two lane dividers mark major traffic arteries. A new bike path for the downtown area is trumpeted, yet a newspaper reporter warns the first day that it is a death trap for cyclists.

So it goes, with mounting injury and mortality rates, not to speak of the massive dent that has become the emblem of the Boston automobile. This situation succeeds in generating intense anger toward, and readiness for, mayhem among the fellow citizenry, as if it were the fault of the street user. Finger-waving admonitions and advertising campaigns on "good driving habits" add to the moralism and further disguise the culprit. It is, in fact, the sins of commission and omission of the decision-makers of urban life, and the social-economic-political system to which they are party and in which they themselves are caught, that constitute the heart of the matter. But as the Boston masses berate and mangle each other, those systems and system-makers continue to go their way unchallenged. We see here in miniature the common plight of middle- and under-class Americans, the self-defeating internecine fray fought among themselves with all its fruitless moralisms and ideologies—and the technocratic agents of dehumanization emerging unscathed from the battle.

of the "principalities and powers" that enslave the spirit as well as the body. Liberation means the ennoblement of our finer sensibilities. And most of all it signifies the control over one's own life, the capacity to choose the future freely.

In the biblical story the world already begins to taste this dream in the exodus from slavery of a small Near Eastern tribe, and the appearance in its midst of a Liberator. The lot of men does not have to be slavery to pain and death, tyranny, and dependency. From Moses to Christ the vision of freedom receives historical confirmation and generates both a hope for and mandate toward the freeing of prisoners. And that hope and mandate have to do with the breaking of the shackles of slaves wherever they may be found—in ghetto or suburb, among middle-aged blue-collar whites as well as among oppressed minorities.

Reconciliation

Liberation as a value does not stand in azure isolation. To be human is to be free *from* in order to free *for*. To be human is to be free to be together. Shalom—unity, wholeness, peace—is the goal of liberation.

The biblical glimpse of the world's fruition is one in which peace is made and all things are finally reconciled. The perennial estrangements among men, between man and nature, within nature, and between man and God are overcome. The wolf lies down with the lamb, swords are beaten into ploughshares, the child puts her hand over the viper's den, the anger of God is turned away. Rehumanization is the repossession, the re-knitting of those ruptured bonds for which an alienated world is made, the free choosing of a life together with nature, man, and God.

Within the Christian tradition the aperture through which we see this vision of wholeness is the man Jesus. As he is our Liberator, so he is our peace. In his person and work, the unities for which humans are destined are manifest. Foretastes of the kingdom come in the neighbor love he taught and lived, and in the horizontal and vertical fractures he healed. That these things could happen in our history and that the promise could be made in those events that "even greater things will you do" are again both the hope and the call to act toward a reconciled and liberated humanity.

Alienated Dreams

The visions of liberation and reconciliation are already present in the ethos of middle America, but in an estranged form, one that militates against its very humanity. Let us examine a few of the secular and religious versions of this extrapolation of freedom and shalom.

The kind of hostility toward established institutions that is represented by right-wing movements is often rooted in a populist urge to be rid of distant architects of one's destiny. As we shall explore in chapter 5, the Wallace phenomenon drew massive response from blue-collar communities because of the conviction that government, banks, the press, industry, and the courts were in collusion with minority groups seeking to advance their own interests at the expense of others. While calculating politicians and vicious hatemongers exploited these anxieties, the fears were tied up with genuine aspirations toward liberation from the technocratic powers that be. To disengage this quest for self-determination from its captivity to racist and reactionary demagoguery is one of the critical challenges to the new breed of political leadership in the seventies.

The flag cult is also a striking example of covert liberation motifs. Purportedly a demonstration of patriotism, the flag decal is manifestly a code language which rebukes the assumed disrupters of "the American way of life." But under its hostile display lies a more poignant meaning. It is a distress signal run up to alert society to the presence of "forgotten Americans." Like the chant that has resounded in countless southern black marches, it is shouting, "I am somebody." Again, strategies for the seventies will fare ill if they do not see below the level of obvious chauvinism to the cries of pain and quest for co-liberation that prompt the jingoistic sights and sounds.

A related expression of alienated dreams is found in the popular religious life of many middle Americans, often found in tandem with the aforementioned secular phenomena. We are dealing here with a continuum that runs from the astrology columns of Jeane Dixon, read avidly by a large number of working-class wives, through the lower-middle-class Billy Graham devotee, to the aging suburban practitioner of Norman Vincent Pealism. Throughout this spectrum can be heard the wistful refrain of liberation, the dream of freedom from want, disease, fear, and insecurity.

Astrology for the middle American housewife trades upon many of the same anxieties that make it popular with some members of the counterculture. The latter, faced with an uncertain future controlled by inscrutable technocratic powers, finds in astrology a way to outmaneuver the Pentagon: there is a design to which even that principality is accountable, and even a VLP can discern its secrets and arrange his life accordingly. With the housewife, it is the day-to-day uncertainties of life in a mill town whose gods of automation seem to propel the worker and his family through unpredictable boom-and-bust cycles and press them to quest for ways to take charge of their own lives. To have control over the astrological forces in back of these penultimate historical surges promises freedom.

Conventional pietism and positive thinking offer similar ways of coping for the more acculturated middle classes. Here freedom from tribulations and powerlessness is sought either by demoting daily life and promoting otherworldly terrain to a position of prominence, or by promising religious techniques for "successful living." Thus the dreams of liberation are nursed along in alienated form.

In the theme of peace we find another constant in middle American piety. Peace of soul, peace of mind, peace of heart— the recent history of the *Reader's Digest,* the magazine that presses its candidacy as scripture for middle Americans, is encompassed in these slogans. They represent the middle American thirst for shalom, frustrated in the outer world and therefore sought for in the inner world, or at best the interpersonal world. The interiorization of religion among the silent majority again runs parallel to the turn inward currently popular in some sections of the counterculture, a phenomenon we explore in chapter 7. In both cases experiences of dehumanization in the hurly-burly arenas of political, economic, and social life prompt flight to the quiet sanctuaries of the soul.

The postwar boom in church life in the United States is not unrelated to the middle American's effort to come to terms with the dehumanizing forces in society, and his dreams of both liberation and reconciliation. Institutional religion provided John Doe a chance to get back his name and his face, albeit within a very limited sector of his culture. In the lay-oriented and grass-roots style of American church life—although it frequently trivialized its participatory democracy by funneling its members' talents into working on the planning committee for the summer picnic, ushering every other Sunday morning, and haggling over whether the parsonage needs a new roof—people did experience some control over their future. And further, within its caring community—the concept of koinonia, fellowship, ranked higher as a priority in the church of the fifties—there was provided a buffer against the depersonalizing current in the wider world.

Again, the similarity to the counterculture is interesting, although the latter's quest for freedom "to do one's own thing," and for community, takes the more radical direction of the participatory commune. Sadly, the same alienated dream is courted by both. The quest for a utopia on the margins of society aborts the major task of building social structures which embody that mirror for all the hopes of liberation and reconciliation. That one might lead to the other is always a possibility, just as the experience of democracy within the congregations of the left wing of the Reformation planted the seeds for political change in Great Britain. Certainly it is the task of the responsible visionary to facilitate that growth outward and to open, as well, the ideological and ecclesiastical prisons in which the dreams of freedom and shalom have been left to waste and die.

Realities

While the fundamental orientation points for humanization of middle America are liberation and reconciliation, it must be remembered that their locus is in the future, and for the religious believer in the Absolute Future. The New Humanity is a transcendent vision that cannot be domesticated. In that lies its provocative power, for it always draws us beyond the givens and never lets us rest content with partial and ambiguous realizations of it in our time and history. Its fragmentary character is bound up with the finiteness and radical evil that pervade our life on earth.

The fact of our finitude means that the vision of perfect freedom possible in a transcendent kingdom must be qualified on our terrain because of the presence of many competing claims of liberation. The finiteness of air means that no industry, auto operator, or homeowner is free to put uncontrolled amounts of waste into the atmosphere. Freedom has its limits in the freedom of others. The ideal of control over one's future—always a goal that lures us toward the enlargement of the maneuvering room of mankind—is qualified in our world of contingency by the liberation rights of others and the healing needs of an exhaustible environment.

The set of reality factors that has particular bearing on our analysis of middle America has to do less with finitude and more with the radical evil that trails our pilgrimage toward visionary goals. In the classic language of the Christian tale the fundamental realities upon which the dreams of men and God are shattered are sometimes described as "sin, death, and the devil." The task of demythologizing involves locating meanings in our contemporary experience that point to what the ancient code language was attempting to express. While secular words do not exhaust the richness of the religious myth, particularly its transcendent referents, they can catch some of the insight in understandable contemporary terms. What might the trinity of evil mean for the task of rehumanization?

Death

Death is the breech of the dreams of liberation and reconciliation. Death is dehumanization. While we now enter a period of growing discontent with the death-dealing social powers that attack middle Americans, many illusions yet remain about their extent, and there is little clarity about their source. Reaching for a few crumbs from the tables of the affluent, and diverted from an awareness of their plight by alienated dreams and other engrossing opiates, the silent majority does not yet fully grasp the depth of the crisis. As the capacity to deal with our physical mortality is in direct proportion to our willingness to look honestly at it, so overcoming dehumanization bears a direct relation to our readiness to look it squarely in the face. Thus "consciousness-raising" becomes a reality task for middle America, much as it has been for other dispossessed peoples who have been lulled into believing that "things are really not so bad after all." Consciousness-raising entails precise identification of the maladies of dehumanization in the day-to-day life of middle America, and the location of the sources of social death at the technocratic control centers. And it involves as well experiments in new life.

Sin

Located at the center of human freedom is the self-aggrandizing surge inimical to nature, man, and God. A sober regard for this self-will that edges toward a will-to-power over others is a central conviction in the Christian understanding of man. And the appreciation of the stubbornness of the imperialism that parasites upon the will of man and his institutions is crucial for making one's way out of the places of death.

There are many faces of sin. Each has a relevance to the struggle for rehumanization.

The will to overpower grows in proportion to the accumulation of power. In assessing who its foe is, therefore, middle America must ask where the agglomerations of power are located. Sobriety about the corruptibility of near-absolute power will also prompt consideration of how that power can be dispersed. Wisdom about self-regarding impulses will underscore the dangers of technocratic elites about which the forgotten American is now angry and apprehensive, but bumbling in his efforts to deal with it. Further, an understanding of the imperialism-power partnership will help the middle American to see the unproductivity of the energies spent in complaining about the activities of the powerless. In fact, realism will prompt him to contemplate alliances with other powerless groups, alliances of the fellow-dehumanized which can alone muster the strength to provide centers of countervailing power necessary to deal with the technocratic monoliths.

To grasp the depth and stubbornness of human perversity is to be wary of too-easy assumptions about the vulnerability of power centers and their readiness to be moved by moral or rational suasion. Morality and reason regularly become the tools and smoke screens of vested interests. In fact, there seems to be a built-in need for establishments to justify themselves in terms of righteous and rational declamations. Reason and morality slide perennially into rationalization and ideology. Provisional wariness about centralization of power is confirmed by this realization of its capacity for self-deception, and the will to give righteous accreditation to its self-interest. This wisdom makes even clearer the importance of developing checks on massive power from the outside and gives added weight to the quest for coalitions that will provide that power.

The other side of this coin is the need for the powerless among minority groups to realize that their own struggle is bound up with that of the middle American. If power grows not out of the gun barrel but out of the broad social consensus described by Hannah Arendt and examined further in chapter 6, then aggrieved peoples must make their breakthroughs by tapping the middle American resources necessary for that momentum.

"What drives middle Americans to the barricades?" They are not goaded into action by appeals to their good nature, any more than the technocrat is moved by moral and rational exhortation. As the self-regarding constants have to be checked and challenged in the technocrat, they have to be mobilized against dehumanization in the middle American. Just as self-interest wedded to inordinate power becomes a source of tyranny, so self-regard mated to the struggle of the powerless can become an instrument of justice. Thus raising the consciousness of dehumanization among middle Americans is more than a general act of benevolence or an appeal to benevolence; it is grounded in the knowledge that self-concern is the most effective way of generating the power that will effect significant social change.

The perils of a naked exploitation of man's self-will, even when it seeks to harness it to social purposes, are manifest in the fanaticism and conceits of the most righteous of causes. A Christian understanding of self-will alerts us to the fact that efforts to use it as a mechanism of social change must be tempered with a somber self-criticism. The powerless as well as the powerful are subject to human perversity. Perversity in the former more often takes the form of the sin of lassitude—the occupational hazard of the medieval monk, acedia, the lethargy that took its toll at midday and hence was nicknamed the midday demon. But the powerless are vulnerable to privateering as well as flight, particularly as their quest for empowerment begins to succeed. Thus the middle American, we middle Americans, must recognize in ourselves the same tendencies we so easily perceive in our foes, subject ourselves to the penitence we expect of others, be prepared to accept the same limitations to and dispersion of our power, and be aware of the temptation of self-righteous fury and rationalization that attend any dragon-slaying venture.

The Devil

The characterization of powerful subrational forces in our psyches and society as "demonic" is a familiar note in such varied thought worlds as those of Paul Tillich, Rollo May, and modern biblical scholarship. We use it here as a tool to relate the third dimension of evil to the rehumanization of middle America.

We have noted that the conventional wisdom of the Left has produced a Manichaean picture in which the modern scene is viewed as a simple contest between the forces of light and the forces of darkness. This view represents a moralism too ready to pass judgment on middle Americans without going to the root of their alienation. We have sought to show that the dehumanization of the silent majority is a major factor in their resistance to important social change, and in particular their anger with the young, the black, and the poor. The putdown get uptight.

The ugly racism, chauvinism, and moralism found among many middle Americans cannot be minimized or excused. Such attitudes and behavior are demonic, "of the devil," and must be confronted and defeated. What is to be rebuked, however, is not the persons, but the principalities and powers that have possessed them. Middle Americans have been invaded by strong subrational and psychological currents. Rather than writing off whole blocs of our fellow citizens, we must confront and overcome occupying powers. It is not the destruction of persons but the exorcism of powers that will both honor the humanity of middle Americans and free us from stereotypes that would impede the coalition of the dehumanized so necessary for social change in the seventies. And to rebuke the demon is to attack it at its source: in the dehumanizing attitudes and patterns of the technocracy.

Vision and Reality

Visionary realism keeps warm its passion for liberation and reconciliation but will ask about the conditions which facilitate these dreams. It will not evade questions of power or shy away from the harnessing of self-interest. Its realism will remind it that the purest causes of the sixties were never as untainted as the visionary rhetoric of those times pretended. Nor will the new thrusts of the seventies be any less free of corruptibility. The sobriety about treasure in earthern vessels must be mated to a humility appropriate to one's own blurred visions and mixed motives. Thus one struggles to live toward the New Commonwealth by the grace of the Light up ahead, and live with one's own war upon that same kingdom by the mercy of its King.

In this section we try to humanize the issues that confront middle America by looking into "faces along First Street," the real people that live in Mill Town, U.S.A. The focus is on a specific problem and on a current mood, both of which take us further into the challenge of rehumanization. The study of blue-collar work and play was produced for a national conference on "leisure and the quality of life" sponsored by the American Institute of Planners and the American Association for Health, Physical Education and Recreation. The probe of right-wing incursions into Mill Town was occasioned by a return visit to old Pittsburgh stamping grounds during the civil-rights ferment of the sixties.

Chapter 4
WORK AND PLAY
IN MILL TOWN

One of the ironies in the massive literature on leisure is the painful, sweaty earnestness with which the inquiry is executed. Deadpan philosophers deliver themselves of finely honed arguments and carefully documented tomes on playfulness. Planners preach with distended forehead veins on how we must learn to enjoy ourselves.

We need responsible research about this exciting new frontier. But there ought to be some connection between the message and the medium. The knob-knuckled old Puritan may be having the last laugh after all as he peers down from the heavenly delights of Elysium at the five "working groups" in a "conference on leisure."

But we are going to try to outfox, and maybe even exorcise, the Puritan ghost this time. The comments that follow will be offered leisurely, with the accent on imagination, the play of ideas, even a little storytelling. Oddly enough, some say this is the way the most serious of subjects ought to be treated. Physicist Ian Barbour speaks about imagination and speculation as critical components of the scientific method. Social radical Ernst Bloch ruminates on the importance of daydreaming as a way of calling into question the status quo. Herman Kahn and his future-researchers brainstorm in their think-tanks about the Not Yet. Does it have to be added that creative mind-blowing can only go on when some solid nourishment in ideas and hard data is fed into the exercise?

The reflections that follow on the ethics of work and leisure are rooted in the thinking and doing of some of the giants in the field—Huizinga, deGrazia, Pieper, Corita. They try to hook in with the kind of thing planners are reading—the *New Journal of Leisure Research* put out by the National Recreation and Park Association—and the kind of frontline experimentation planners are engaged in—Banner Day at the Civic Center Mall in Los Angeles.

Definitions

Whole books are written on the meaning of the word leisure. Such activity can be a kind of game itself, and therefore can hardly be criticized by those who believe in play. But with due regard for Huizinga's distaste for spoilsports, we shall cut the Gordian knot with some working definitions that seem to make sense in a planning context. We shall use free time as a descriptive and leisure as a normative word. *Free time* is discretionary time, what is available for choosing use by the body or mind or spirit, or any combination of these, when not absorbed by employment or the execution of such other necessary functions as eating, sleeping, housework, shopping, traveling to and from work, and the like. Note: sometimes there is free time for the mind or spirit even when the body is occupied, as in traveling to work, shopping, eating. *Leisure* is the restorative, creative use of free time. Leisure is the ennoblement of the discretionary. When free time is utilized and celebrated so that personal, social, and natural values accrue, then it becomes leisure. What those values are we shall presently explore.

G. Candilis, in a recent American Institute of Planners meeting, helpfully isolated three functions of leisure: relaxation, entertainment, and development. We use this trinity here, adding a few nuances. Relaxation we understand to mean rest, the slowing down of the self's motor, the ministration to fatigue. Entertainment we interpret as play. Play is the suspension of the business of living in order to do something "just for the fun of it." It can be solitary, like stamp-collecting, or communal, like a football game. It can involve the body (as in a race), the mind (as in a crossword puzzle), or the spirit (as in a festival, religious or secular).

Development is a creative use of free time which, while not geared to the necessities of life, is devoted to expanding vistas, personal and social. It's what happens when an individual cultivates his latent artistic talent. But it is also what happens when that same person uses this gift in a settlement house or for the celebration of the city. Has the Puritan crept back into the inner sanctum of leisure in our conception of development? To honor leisure and to struggle for its right to be, yet not include the purposive dimensions, is to make leisure and hedonism synonymous. They are not. Leisure is the mother of politics and education, as well as play and contemplation, as Pieper seeks to show.

Faces Along First Street

Central to the ethical question is the effect of an idea or structure on persons. In pursuit of a leisure ethic, therefore, and in line with the imagination-oriented methodology for which we have opted, let's take a trip down the main street of an American community, Mill Town, U.S.A. We select a working-class community for a couple of reasons. The problems we face show up here vividly, for one. For another, the worker and his family represent the leisure masses which a new ethic must finally penetrate. And for another, it's that sector of society which the writer knows a little better than some others.

As we arrive at First Street and Grant Avenue, we find Sam— "Turkey Sam" to his friends from the old country—sitting with his pensioner cronies at their daily haunt on the sidewalk bench under the bank clock. The old men are not playing cards today or watching the miniskirts on their way to work. The word is out that the Redevelopment Authority plans have been voted on, and "they" are going to tear the bank down and rearrange the downtown map.

"What's gonna happen to Bill's candy store, where we bought our papers all our life and played the numbers? They gonna get rid of our bench too, I betcha. Parking lots all over the place. People rushing around all over the place. The big boys push us out of the mill, now they push us off the street. Whataya gonna do?"

Sam's wife died years ago, and he's been living with one of his sons in a suburban housing development. He gets on the bus to come downtown every morning because he feels like a fifth wheel around the house. His whole life had been his job at the mill, with no time or inclination for hobbies. So he clings to the fragments of past reality that he can piece together from the comradeship with his retired fellow workers. In addition to reminiscing at bench and bar, he watches TV (when the grandchildren or mom and dad aren't glued to their programs), reads the obituaries, and visits an old friend in the hospital. Now what's in store for me, he wonders. The kids aren't going to want me underfoot. Off to the old folks' home?

We meet our next steel-city citizen, Steve, coming out of the gas station on the corner. He's rushing home to get ready for the 3 to 11 turn at the mill. But hasn't he been pumping gas at Howdy's Esso all morning? Right, but that's his second job. Steve moonlights twenty hours a week to get enough extra money to send his boy to college. He says he doesn't want any son of his to have to work in the blast furnace all his life the way he did. Then, too, a little extra cash in your pocket never hurt anyone. So Steve's existence is the daily trek from job to job, interspersed now and then with a late-night beer while slumped in front of a late-night movie on TV. Yes, there's that hunting trip with the guys on the opening day of deer season and the evening off with the wife at the shopping center, but all that's on the margins. Life is work. What else?

Look, there goes Mabel, dashing across the street right in front of a car. She must be headed for the lodge hall; there's a big to-do there tonight. As "queen" she'll have to see if the seating is all right for the guests and all the menus are out. With the kids in school now, Mabel can't stand just sitting around the house with nothing to do. She had plans to help out at the hospital as a nurses' aid, but that never quite materialized because there just wasn't enough time, what with the lodge responsibilities, Monday at the hairdresser, Tuesday night bingo, Wednesday card parties at the Volunteer Fireman's Hall, and so on. Last week her husband, who sometimes wonders whether it all adds up to anything as he babysits night after night, put a little poem on her mirror:

Busy: An Epitaph

Here lies a poor woman who was always busy
She belonged to ten clubs that rendered her dizzy
Read Browning and Clowning, Whitman and DeVries
Served at church suppers, shone at luncheons and teas
Golfed and Kodaked, tried bridge and Canasta
Was President of the guild and chairman of the fiesta
Her children she saw only once in awhile
Her husband signed checks and tried hard to smile
One day on her schedule she found an hour that was free
The shock was too great and she died instantly.
Anonymous

Duke is nineteen, a high school dropout. His laughter booms through the door of Andy's, where he's playing a lively game of pool with the boys. Duke's been laid off at the mill for three months now because of the scarcity of orders, and because he's third helper on the open hearth with almost no seniority. So he's just been hanging around at Andy's, over at the gas station chewing the rag with Steve, working on his '61 Ford, then cruising through town at night picking up some girls, and off now and then to that secluded lane in the country for a game of "chicken" with the gang. He knows the cops have been watching Andy's lately, looking for the stuff stolen from the jewelry store and for the "acid" being sold at the high school. They haven't got a thing on him, though—yet.

Duke thinks the police would like to nail him anyway, on general principles. He heard a couple of them talking to one of the downtown merchants on the corner last week about the "freeloaders" when he and his mother were on the way to the welfare office to get their check. It seems as if being out of work is the worst sin you could commit. And sometimes he even gets to despising himself when he's off work.

So here are four people with free time, but little or no leisure. How come?

There is a villain in the piece. It's a little hard to track him down because he comes in different sizes and shapes. We see him in the life-style of a Sam who never knew anything meaningful but his work. He pops up in the blueprints for the new downtown complex that designs out of existence Sam's bench, candy store, and friends, sending him back to an inhospitable suburbia to end up in next year's obits. Our culprit surfaces in an economy that makes Steve moonlight to get his kid into college, and lets him numb himself to fatigue in a grade C, 2 A.M. movie. He changes costume to meet us in Mabel's frenzied free time, and in Duke's enforced "free" time. And to cap it off, we hear the echoes of his voice in the corner conversation that whispers, "Workless is worthless" as Duke passes by.

We are talking about old Mr. Work-Worth himself, born four hundred years ago when the Protestant Ethic married the Spirit of Capitalism. While a new technology has spilled us into another era, the old gentleman has not yet had the grace to realize that he's had it. He continues to run the show in Mill Town as if nothing had happened since John Calvin wrote his *Institutes* and the Dutch merchants cut their trade loose from the kings and princes. Work-Worth is the cultural premise that now takes its toll on the Sams, Stevens, Mabels, and Dukes.

But let's watch for a misstep here as we haul Work-Worth before the new leisure's bar of judgment. We are not talking only about an attitude, an idea rooted in a new secularized Calvinist ideology. The attitude has crystallized into an environment of steel and concrete structures and of economic, political, and social structures which are no less real. While Work-Worth has to be routed on the attitudinal front, the ethical task includes the effort to pry him loose from the control of structures as well. A work world that forces Steve to moonlight and throws Duke into the streets is also part of the problem of leisure. And so is a play world that has nothing to offer but a parking lot for a pensioner, dulling TV fare to the exhausted, and a fantasy queenship to the bored.

The multiple fronts on which the leisure struggle has to be waged suggest that the aborning alliance between ethicists and planners is a right move. Ethicists are beginning to realize that the most scintillating ideas which are not embodied in structures cut very little ice. You cannot preach or write books at people about getting off the work kick and on into a leisure era without providing a physical environment in which free time can be transformed into leisure. And even if you succeed in getting those pleasant parks, carefully contoured landscapes, and celebrative cityscapes, Steve, Duke & Co. can't appreciate them if their bodies and minds are wracked with exhaustion or despair because of work patterns. So structures are very much matters of ethics.

Meanwhile, planners are asking the ethical questions, and they see that the best-laid plans can be frustrated by captivity in high places and low to the wiles of Work-Worth—"When you've seen one tree, you've seen them all." And more, planners are challenging in their profession what Max Lerner in *America as Civilization* calls "the technician mentality" by interpreting their role as change agents. The recent American Institute of Planners Task Force Restatement of AIP Goals and Objectives will be welcomed by many working at urban issues. Goal 1: *"Aggressively lead in social change.* Assume aggressive leadership in achieving societal change leading to the solution of urban problems."

Is it possible that urban planners, who too often accommodate the designs of the technocracy, can join the ranks of those fighting back against dehumanization? Is an alliance possible between the white-collar planner and the blue-collar worker?

From Work-Worth to Leisure-Worth

Interlaced with the old technology was a work ethic that served and sanctioned industrial culture for centuries. As an accelerating new technology opens up expanses of discretionary time (free and forced) before which the old ideology is helpless and in fact destructive, we must find a guide to take us over horizons only dimly perceived. What are the qualifications of Leisure-Worth that must replace Work-Worth?

Let's start with basics. What is life for? What is leisure for? There are certain motifs, ideas, even words that capture the imagination, speak to the deepest needs, turn on the brightest spirits, and sum up the finest sensibilities of a generation. Shalom is one of those ideas and words. Whether it appears on a medallion, in a UN speech, a papal announcement, or an ad for an airline, it strikes deep chords of hope and aspiration in the modern soul. Shalom is the beating of swords into ploughshares, the healing of bodies and minds. It is putting together what is torn in self and society, nature and history. It is what makes human life human, nature's life natural, and the divine life divine. And we shall maintain here that it is the quality that transforms free time into leisure.

Leisure, then, is shalomed discretionary time. Let's see how that fits into our preliminary tripartite formulation. Relaxation is the knitting together of the physical and emotional cleavages that express themselves in fatigue, the running down and falling apart of the self's engines. What is shattered is moved toward wholeness when relaxation is made possible.

Play is also food for the starving soul and society, according to Huizinga. It is an ingredient in cultures that keeps them sane. Why? Men need a certain point in their lives which is not controlled by pragmatism, where they do not ask how such-and-such contributes to the business of securing food, clothing, and shelter. In these preserves we cultivate a certain nonchalance toward the rat race. Our focus is out yonder, doing something non-productive, for its own sake. Both Huizinga and Pieper note the striking similarity (and, for that matter, the historic connection) between play and worship. Both teach us to treat relative things relatively. Both are instruments of a shalom which knits up the raveled sleeves of care that sleep and relaxation cannot touch.

Playfulness also can make bearable and even exhilarating the sounds and sights of the urban world, as Corita Kent has demonstrated in her pop art. Play that rearranges the environment so that we can probe its deeper meaning, smile at it, laugh at it, unites us with our world, and is therefore shalom.

Development is a shalom category because it seeks to close the gap between potentiality and actuality and between actuality and ideality. Does the self have a musical bent? Development is leisure that brings it to be. Does society have black-white, young-old alienations that sunder it? Development is leisure oriented to reconciliation. Is nature shredded by foul air, polluted streams, devastated forests? Ecological development is leisure used to heal a groaning creation.

Leisure therefore, is worthful because it embodies and facilitates shalom in its three functions of relaxation, play, and development. But let us try to refine our leisure ethic even further. The highest kind of leisure is that which exercises what is uniquely human in the interests of shalom.

The quality that makes man man, the capacity that distinguishes him within the natural order is his freedom. Man can take charge of his own life. He can choose, seize his own future. The life of man is human, therefore, to the degree that man exercises the capacity of self-determination and to the degree that his institutions leave him maneuvering room to exercise it. One of the current struggles in our society is the surge forward of the VLP's (Very Little Persons) to claim their humanity. That kind of liberation struggle is much to the fore in our society. The young, the poor, the black—so long submerged by political, educational, and social autocracies—now rise to claim their "say" in things, their right to have a voice in their own destiny. Liberation means participation. To participate is to be a man.

It is the same with leisure. Participative leisure humanizes.

When the self climbs down from the spectator's perch in the grandstand to be a player, then genuine play happens. When development involves, and particularly when it involves in the interests of men taking more charge of their own lives, the human level of leisure rises.

If leisure is good and a liberative shalom is its polestar, how can the worlds of Sam, Steve, Mabel, and Duke be restyled and redirected in light of these values?

New Attitudes and Environments
for First Street Citizens

Sam's basic leisure problem is no longer fatigue, although it was during his twelve-hour, six-day work week in the old days. He needs to be convinced of leisure's importance. Perhaps it will only be the Sams-to-come with whom this can be adequately done, that is, during the work years themselves. Society must cultivate a philosophy of leisure that meets them in the newspaper editorial, from the pulpit, and on the subway poster. As the hours decline at work, the sabbatical becomes widespread in the factory, and the retirement age drops, industry—in cooperation with public and other private agencies—must provide the new Sams with leisure counselors that will help them exorcise the demon of Work-Worth.

All this sounds like a low-priority luxury in a society with so many clamoring needs. But one thinks of the pensioners who are not so fortunate as Sam sitting under the bank clock, the thousands who die shortly after retirement because they have nothing more to live for. The Hutschnecker studies and other data like them have strongly suggested that deterioration and death are correlates of retirement because the will to live was tied to society's definition of worth: work.[1] The commitment to a new ethic of leisure and its implementation through counseling and communication may be life-and-death matters for the aged.

What about an environment for the living Sams commensurate with the needed new attitude toward leisure? Sam needs to play. Playing means more than checkers under the bank clock. He needs to play with ideas, the passing parade, with the sun, sky, and trees, with the color, sounds, and smell of the city. He needs to Corita-ize his surroundings. To do that he requires the materials and the setting. It can't be done in a parking lot, and it won't be done if he is evicted from his urban "home." He must be where the action is, and where he can be with those with whom he can play the game.

If the intimacy of the bank bench must fall under the wrecker's ball, can the rebuilders of center city make a playground for Sam? Can it be reborn alongside the fountain in the new civic mall? In the gardens of the new under-cover shopping center throbbing with the life of all sorts and conditions of men? Will there be opportunity for Sam to visit the old cronies in the retirement home or the convalescent residence because they are within walking distance? Can he make it to the hospital, the library, and the church too? In this playground, where he will spend the greater part of his time, will he learn something about the natural beauty he never had time for on his three-shift schedule and the urban beauty of which he never took notice on his way to work? And can he get to the gardens and the walks, and have the chance to look up and around at the city horizons, without being asphyxiated and harassed by a traffic flow that robs the most delightful and intimate settings of their fulfillment?

So far we've been talking about an environment that will serve and stretch Sam's leisure. For too long we have assumed that all the aged need are the things we can give them. Let them also "do their thing" for shalom! Let leisure be development as well as play, the matching of Sam's capabilities to social needs, a mating whose by-product will be the satisfaction of having done something to make the world a better place to live in. In fact, can we take Sam's need to feel that he is a contributing member of society, unhook it from its factory-work context, and hitch it to the vehicle of social service? To do that we must put within range of his urban habitat opportunities for this kind of servanthood. Do we have a clue in the public-school programs that harness the time and talents of senior citizens for tutoring and "TLC" in the mass educational factories of today, where there is very little staff time for the kind of personal care so desperately needed? How many public and private agencies could use Sam to man the serving barricades!

Sam's appetite could be whetted at the sight of the wrecking ball. Will it be?

As we had to begin several steps back from the immediate environment of Sam, so too with Steve. Leisure cannot become anything more than marginal for him until some of his work problems are resolved. People who are concerned about leisure for the worker must interest themselves also in such things as the grant and loan programs for colleges and the wage contracts of factory employees.

But Steve might just continue to eat up all his spare time at Howdy's, not because he lacks for basics, but because he has entered the race of keeping up with the Joneses. For this idolatry of the affluent, before whose golden calf blue-collar workers are getting the means to bow today, there is only one cure: a new set of value priorities. Shalom must unseat the goddess of getting-ahead.

Until that day comes, what can be done to entice Steve off the clogged highways of Work-Worth and onto the wooded paths of Leisure-Worth? For one thing, we can put a few pointers along the freeway and lure him away from the traffic. OK, so he does have to come downtown to Howdy's and to the mill. What assaults his mind as he rides the bus or decides to walk the river road, or his nostrils as he passes the docks, or his eardrums as he goes through the shopping center or turns on his transistor? It does not have to be the drab, the sordid, the noxious, or the frenetic. Planning could build in rest for the exhausted body and contemplation for the drained mind by the contours and colors seen from the bus window, the designs that catch his eye in the ads, and the seats within. It might replace the smell of trash burning and river pollution with breathable air and the scent of trees. How much could be done to mellow the dissonance with a BBC 3 type of option on the transistor or shopping center loudspeaker would be hard to say. But it would be worth a try. And while we're at it, we might borrow from British "telly" to improve our midnight horrors.

If we try to take on that river, it would mean more than a pleasant scene on the way to work. Steve would not have to wait for that yearly weekend trip to Canada to take his son fishing. It is interesting to speculate what ready access to restful leisure opportunities might be to the generation gap and family unity —not only the fishing trip with the kids, but the regular family outing in the green-belt park, and even the chance for such not-very-proletarian sports as that made possible by a nearby ski run.

What makes Mabel run? Perhaps Mr. Work-Worth is at it again. Labor-saving devices release Mabel from grandmother's chores but not her ideology. She still has to prove to herself that she is doing her bit, justifying her existence by "working" at fever pitch at play. The opinion-molders and new ethicists have their job cut out with the Mabels.

Yet the rat race could be more than grandmother's influence. It might be that the physical and social environment is so profoundly unsatisfying that flight seems the only course. Urban sights and sounds take their toll of Mabel, too. Does it have to be the case that opportunities for genuine culture cannot be within easy reach of the worker's family? For all the damage the old steel baron Carnegie did to his workers, he tried to make amends in the leisure sphere by his famous steel-town "libraries" —a smorgasbord of books, swimming pool, clubrooms, classes, community service opportunities. True, the workers were too worn out and demoralized to take full advantage of this rich fare. But Mabel's exhaustion is to a large extent self-inflicted; people today could be truly benefited if similar opportunities were available, updated in style and texture.

The voluntary association must take its share of the blame for Mabel's wearying round of inconsequentia. The lodge, the club, the church do not have to be exercises in navel-gazing and trivia. They can be development at its most purposive. They can serve Mabel with mind-stretching, and they can give her ways of serving her city that are more visionary and selfless than "going through the chairs." In our planning context it would mean that planners themselves will seek out allies in their efforts toward "aggressive leadership in achieving societal change" among Mabel's voluntary associations. I think of a town of a hundred Mabels, along with a few Sams, Steves, and other such odd types as college professors, Community Action Program workers, seminary students, and planners who have banded together to start a local independent newspaper. When a county planner heads the task force responsible for the recreation issue of the paper, and gets Mabel to use her photographic talents to take pictures of the dump in the Seventh Ward that could be used for a tot lot and the polluted pond that could be used for kids' fishing and swimming, then we are in a different ball game. Leisure becomes participative, healing—life, not death.

Society has a convenient target for its frustrations in the Dukes of our time. You've heard the refrain: "Look, he hangs around the poolroom with a lot of the same ilk. They're all too lazy to get a job. They have a free ride at our expense on our hard-earned tax money. They're all criminal types anyway, stealing, taking drugs, smashing up innocent people on the highways."

Free time in the life of a Duke is indeed an explosive mix. The "threat of the new leisure" is clearest of all among the young who have vast new expanses of time to kill, or be killed with. But the simplistic moralism of the affluent will never do as a diagnosis. The roots of the problem go deeply into the soil in which the moralists prosper and the Dukes wither.

Discretionary time which is enforced is not fertile terrain in which to grow the spirit. To the degree that Duke is flotsam washed onto the sands of unemployment and back into the sea again by economic tides, he is hardly a candidate for creative leisure. Add to that the Work-Worth philosophy that greets Duke from the pages of his first-grade reader to the sulky face at the unemployment office window. and you get not only social defeat but personal self-hate.

"But it's his own fault. He's a dropout."

Thereby hangs a tale. It has to do with new educational insights that increasingly understand Duke as a push-out rather than a dropout, the victim of a callous and obsolete system.

Again, we find that those who care about fulfilling new leisure have to begin well behind the designing of parks and playgrounds, in the recesses of the human soul and the structures of society where the survival and growth of the seeds of leisure will be first determined. We must challenge Work-Worth's control of the classroom and the mind of the unemployment officer, and those whose taxes reluctantly and penuriously fund them. But we must ask serious questions as well about the growing reservoir of young humanity from the ghettos and the mill towns, untapped and untrained for work in a cybernated age. The passing of Work-Worth must bring economic adjustments which see to it that society does not penalize those for whom it cannot provide work, and in fact honors their dignity by overhauled welfare and assured-income procedures.

Will Duke have his problems solved by planners, churchmen, and humanitarians pitching in to change structures and ideologies? This will help. But Duke himself is a crucial key to his own healing. When he decides that his humanity is being threatened by his flotsam destiny, and when he determines that his children will not suffer the same fate, then there is hope. Thus, Duke attacks the imprisoning aspect of his leisure at a critical point when he joins a welfare union to challenge ideas and arrangements which are captive to Work-Worth. He does it again when he and his neighbor struggle for schools that will not produce another generation of push-outs. And when Duke throws his participative and shaloming energies into such developmental projects, he will begin to discover some leisure by-product satisfactions and an open secret of the great religions: "Seek first the kingdom . . . and these things will be added to you."

For the Dukes we want the intimate downtowns, the green belts, and the BBC 3's. But until he is freed in soul and structure, these will be like Carnegie's well-meant libraries. For the planner, the call cannot be clearer than that issued by the AIP Task Force, the call to "advocacy": "Working for the poor and minority groups at the local level through the exercise of our professional function."

The Cost and Joy

As planners move closer to the ethical question in work and leisure, and as they get involved in such things as advocacy, two observations come to the mind of this ethicist and agitator.

1. Things can get sticky with the powers that be. I'm sure you can supply your own examples of that from your experience— prophets with honor, except in their own homestead. That is the way it is throughout the nation. Take the case of the planner who joined forces with the *Lancaster* (Pa.) *Independent Press* to balance the power of a monopoly press. One month later he got his walking papers.

In the short run there is going to be resistance to planners who move beyond the technician role in order to be "lobbyists for the future." In the long run they will be vindicated, for their struggle for shalom will be seen to be a fight for the future of society itself. But at the moment, get ready for the flak.

2. It's a small step from the prophet's courage to the martyr's complex. If one moves in a variety of urban orbits of the reformist stripe, it soon becomes clear that each thinks it is the only one taking the lumps. Sobriety about what is actually happening comes when one looks around for his allies, finds them, tempers his messianism, and does some shared pushing at the doors that have to be downed.

And surely there is some counsel for this business of taking ourselves too seriously in all our talk here about play. Huizinga shows pretty conclusively that play is the place a culture says, "Really, now, aren't you wound up a little too tight about the whole thing?" And he indicates as well how play and worship meet at this point, feeding the spirit with a certain nonchalance about what goes on in the rush of daily affairs, each teaching us to keep penultimate things penultimate.

For the planner and the preacher who think of their ethical efforts more highly than they ought to, there is some playful advice from two very different sources. Take your pick: "I say that a man must be serious about the serious, and not the other way about. God alone is worthy of seriousness, but man is God's plaything, and that is the best part of him. . . . Life must be lived as play" (Plato). "Why do the nations conspire, and the people plot in vain? The kings of the earth set themselves, and the rulers take counsel together, against the Lord. . . . He who sits in the heavens laughs (Ps. 2:1-4)."

Chapter 5
THE BLUE-COLLAR WHITE
AND THE FAR RIGHT

It was a celebration. The congregation felt it had a lot to be thankful for. It had come a long way from its slum storefront quarters to the little brick colonial in "workingman's paradise," the suburban fringe of this Pittsburgh mill town. And now the mission pastor who had lived through that transitional decade with them was back to give the speech at the festivities. But what a disappointing speech! There were some red faces that night, and even a few red necks.

"Well, he's a right guy. He stuck with me all night at the hospital when our boy was deathly sick. And he helped me find a part-time job when I was laid off at the mill. But him standing up now and saying we have to get with this civil-rights stuff— uh-uh. So what if he just got back from some march on Washington! That's no cause to come here and tell us we got to get mixed up with the colored. They're getting too pushy anyway."

Such comments were common in afterdinner conversation on that celebration day in 1963. Blue-collar types do not hide their feelings under middle-class pleasantries and phony smiles. After ten years of ministry to salty steelworkers and their families, I was used to this kind of bluntness. But it did come as a pain and a shock to hear such outright bigotry from my former parishioners. Had I not got through at all in those earlier years on some terribly basic things?

Alienation

From a more recent vantage point, I can see that their reaction should not have come as so much of a surprise. The full bloom of prejudice that is so manifest in mill-town talk these days was there in seed form years ago. But something else was there too that nursed the seed. And that something should also have been apparent to a pastor who had his congregation answering questionnaires, responding to interviewers, and graciously putting up with being measured by a Lloyd Warner Index of Status Characteristics, all in the interest of finding out what makes Mill Town tick. It was, and is, alienation—as severe, disorienting, and thingifying as that felt by the black, the young, and the poor.

If we are to understand and to deal with the right-wing phenomenon in blue-collar communities, we must go to its roots in the feelings and facts of working-class estrangement. This festering sore requires the same kind of care we have given other wounds on the Jericho road.

"They" is a familiar word in the lexicon of a steel-valley worker. It comes into play in a variety of settings. "They" are the company which is to blame when the mill is shut down for lack of orders, or when a new piece of automated equipment is introduced that eliminates old jobs, or when an explosion occurs and kills a man in furnace 6. But "they" can also be the union when a strike drags on interminably, or when things appear to be decided by "the clique" who regularly attend the meetings of Local 1743. There are times when "they" are the government—national, state, local—that presides over one's destiny in the matter of meat prices, gun ownership, and downtown parking space. And "they" can be the big hospital where one is merely "the ulcer in 304." "They" can even be the church where the priest "runs things as he pleases" and the minister thinks of you as a name on a file card.

There are two components in the dehumanization expressed in the language of estrangement. One is the blue-collar conviction that an individual does not have any control over the forces that shape his life. The Kafka-like castle rules in industry, union, government, commerce, communications, religion, and so on. An alien force manipulates one's future. The worker is a pawn and a puppet.

The other component is just as full of hurt. The autocrat does not really care. The impersonal becomes the depersonal. The worker is a statistic rather than a person, an object rather than a subject. "They do not even know my name."

To be human includes the power of self-determination and the opportunity to participate in relationships of care. From these comes the capacity to love. But the worker is overcome by a sense of powerlessness and by an awareness that the fabric of personal community has been shredded. Could that be why our pleas to love the neighbor often fall on deaf ears? In the 1950's we often heard comments on the apathetic worker. Why didn't he rise up and do something about his alienated lot? The edge of revolt was blunted by a rising standard of living. And, of course, it was an era of general lassitude. If the youth of that time were complacent, then we could not expect much more from the blue-collar worker sunk in his overstuffed chair in front of the TV set.

Nevertheless, something else was at work. Lloyd Warner took note of it when he underscored the prominent role played by the voluntary association in industrial communities. The worker learned to live with alienation by retreat into the private sector of his life. He found balm for his woes in his family, his ethnic community, his clubs, his tavern, and (in some cases) his church. Those were the places where John Doe got back his face and his name, where he "had a say," where he experienced participation and community. What was denied him in the public structures he tasted in the private ones.

But something happened in the 1960's that changed the attitude of blue-collar whites toward their alienation: the human-rights struggle of the blacks. The Negro suffered the same estrangements as the white worker, compounded a hundredfold by economic, political, social, and personal humiliations. But now the black community was not taking it any longer. They struck back at their oppressors.

Crossing a Line

The human-rights revolution of the sixties had at least three effects on blue-collar whites, touching the problem of their alienation.

1. In the mind of the blue-collar worker, the black citizens had "gotten to" the effective centers of cultural change. In fact, as far as he could see from changes in his own existence, "they" were in cahoots with the blacks. As he saw it, strings were pulled that took Negroes off sweeper jobs and put them on the line next to him or, miracle of miracles, in foreman and executive jobs above him. He even heard rumors of preferential hiring which, according to barroom talk, would put him out on the street in favor of the black man. And when he came home

from the frustrations of work, what did he find? "They" were pushing black faces at him through the TV screen which was supposed to be his escape hatch from the harsh realities of daily life. Furthermore, "they" were rearranging his neighborhood so that these "outsiders" could move in, and "they" were conducting social experiments with his kids, moving things around in the schools so that the black could "take over" there too. In all these cultural shifts, it seemed clear to the white worker, "they" were at it again. And, of all things, "they" were giving the Negro the decision-making power and personal recognition he himself so desperately craved.

2. Buried deep in the urban complex, the blue-collar communities and the blue-collar work force made up those frontiers of white society that were most directly affected by the structural changes in patterns of housing, education, and jobs in the 1960's. It is this group—the most vulnerable in terms of sociological and psychological need and the least prepared by training in human relations and education—that we asked to absorb the shock of cultural change.

3. Always alert to what "they" were doing to him, sharp-eyed tavern cynics were quick to note that Mr. Big did not seem very anxious to take part in the social changes he seemed to be engineering. "They" sent their kids to private schools, commuted out of the city to exclusive suburbs at night, sipped their drinks at lily-white country clubs, and could get away from it all at a Colorado ski run or an eastern Mediterranean gambling table. The moral rhetoric spelled out on the editorial pages of slick middle-class magazines did not go down very well with the worker who suspected where the writer was spending his weekends.

The Explosion

The fuel of white racism has been set afire in the streets of Mill Town.

"When the liberals and the intellectuals say the people don't have any sense, they talkin' about us people—they talkin' about the people here. But hell, you can get good solid information from a man drivin' a truck, you don't need to go to no college professor. The fella on the street has got a better mind than these here sissy-britches intellectual morons. . . . These here national politicians like Humphrey and Johnson and Nixon, they don't hang their britches on the wall and do a flyin' jump into 'em every mornin', they put 'em on one britches leg at a time, just like the folks here in Chilton County. Earl Warren on the Supreme Court, he's one of them big Republicans, and he's done more against you 'n' me than anybody else in this country. . . . The Republicans now, they havin' to meet in banks tryin' to figger out what they gonna do about us down here. I'm not talkin' about the good banks of Chilton County or Alabama, I'm talkin' about the Chase National and the Wall Street crowd. . . . The national press now, anything's that bad about yo, guvnuh, oh yes, they gonna run that." [1]

The intellectuals, the politicians, the courts, the bankers, the press—the enemies of the little man. Not the president of Alabama State Teachers, or the Montgomery courthouse steps coterie, or the county seat judge, or the Chilton bank, or the Dogpatch *Bugle*. No, it's the Mr. Bigs. That's where the trouble lies, with those distant architects of our destiny who arrange things to suit their selfish whims.

This catalog of tyranny has been read before by the Birmingham steelworker and the Sunflower County truck driver. It's the same gang he swore at from his TV chair back in the 1950's, the same fellows he tried to forget then at the tavern, in the bowling game, and on the hunting trip. But in the fifties there was nobody to tell it like it is. "And besides they've gone too far this time, what with giving the colored everything."

George Wallace turns them on. Not only does he put into words (in code language on "law and order" that they understand very well) what's on their minds about the blacks and the big shots, but he "treats you like a person." Wallace speaking:

"Yes, yes, I know yo uncle, he works down at H. L. Green's. Tell him hello for us, heunh? He sho is our friend. I saw yawl up the road, I believe, I sho 'preciate yawl bein' with us today, heunh? I 'preciate yawl's suppote, you know Hollis Jackson died. Honey, thank you very much, heunh? Glad to see you—yes, how is yo daughter now? Well, you tell her I been thinkin' about her. Hi, sweetie pie, honey, thank you. Yes, you know, I still miss Mr. Roy. I hear, I understand she was goin' to junior high. 'Cose, her daddy got killed, you know. I sho will. I be glad to shake hands with her. She in the car? . . . I'll be over there in a minute." [2]

George Wallace gave John Doe a face and a name. Or so it seemed to the beleaguered blue-collar white. Wallace struck out at the gray abstraction, the "they" that ran things, and at the black concretion that usurped them. A turn to the Right would straighten out the country. The little spoiler from Alabama would bring down the mighty from their seats and exalt those of low degree.

He didn't—at least not the first time. The warrior was sent scurrying home, deserted by some of his early blue-collar followers. But it may have been more a temporary setback than a total defeat. The "little man" from Alabama did make a comeback and was elected to a new term as governor. And the deep estrangement on which the Wallace phenomenon fed is still very much there in Mill Town, U.S.A., waiting to be exploited again. It is only when the worker's *humanum* is honored in the structures and relationships of the modern industrial world that the right-wing madness will lose its attraction, and the bigotry aimed at black brothers will have some chance of being laid to rest.

Ministry to Blue-Collar Whites

Worker priest, factory chaplain, mill-town parson, storefront minister—there was a time in the not so distant past when these were missionary symbols. The claim and luster of that frontier has faded. No longer can it be said that here is where the wounds of society are the deepest. Gone also is the romantic thesis that the future will be determined by those who "win the soul of the workingman." The relative affluence of blue-collar workers, their decreasing social and political significance due to technological changes and the rise of the white-collar segment, the tarnished image of a labor movement no longer unambiguously aligned with the forces of creative social change—all have served to mute the blue-collar mission mandate.

But for all their lackluster qualities, the blue-collar communities are still, and in some ways more than ever, missionary turf. "Relative affluence" does not cure some very fundamental miseries. That is what the alienated students struggling for a voice in their academic and political future are discovering; that is what Watts's blacks have known for a long time. Together with other estranged sectors of society, the blue-collar workers have been afflicted with a sense of powerlessness. And as they are powerless, they are also loveless—in both senses of the term. The Christian conscience has been sensitized in the sixties to the plight of the dehumanized black, poor, and young. It should be similarly sensitized to the social futility of the blue-collar white.

A fundamental first step is to attempt to establish a genuine presence in the blue-collar world. The church is involved in token fashion in a sprinkling of industrial missions. These kinds of efforts must be greatly increased. But newer forms of ministry must also be explored—forms which facilitate a more nearly complete immersion in and identification with the blue-collar ethos. In this respect there are some lessons to be learned from the church's involvement in the civil-rights movement. Just as the black church served as a vehicle for reclaiming the humanity of its constituents, it may well be that blue-collar congregations—Protestant, Catholic, Orthodox—can be laboratories and launching pads for restoration of worker dignity. The parish covers the whole spectrum of blue-collar humanity—the housewife, the elderly, the young, the employed, the unemployed—and so offers a chance for fuller exposure to the blue-collar world than do solely work-oriented ministries.

A next step is involvement in the struggle for the recovery of the blue-collar *humanum*. Again the surge forward of the black, the poor, and the young gives us helpful models. Participation is a key motif. The individual must find his voice in the institutions that define blue-collar life; that is, he should "have a say" in the industrial mechanism that exercises such a basic influence over blue-collar destinies. What this participation means in a particular milieu will have to be worked out by those who live within that milieu; it cannot be prescribed by ideological blueprints. More and more the student is being given a voice and vote on what was once the faculty committee, and more and more the black poor have a voice not only in their own welfare institutions but also at the council tables of black capitalism. We must ask what this kind of involvement means for institutions with blue-collar constituencies. Hasn't the union already established a worker beachhead in the industrial decision-making process? Perhaps—in principle, at least. But again we must ask some embarrassing questions. Does the union in fact give a voice to the voiceless worker in this or that particular situation? Where bureaucracy and a monolithic structure block the lines of communication and decision, we have not one but two power centers that need to be democratized.

Alongside industry and union there exists an array of community institutions that cry out for the dispersion of power and the surfacing of the industrial VLP's—the schools, political structures, consumerism, communications media, housing, and the like. In whatever occupation he exercises his ministry, the "chaplain" to the industrial communities has his work cut out for him, as surely as the campus chaplain and the black pastor who have served as catalyst and ally in other rehumanizing struggles.

But not only an ally; the industrial chaplain must be a critic-in-residence as well. Because he is part of the fabric of the blue-collar community, he can bring from within the word of judgment and reconciliation that is so desperately needed in those sectors of the white community which are prey to the racism that afflicts the American soul. Black militants are telling conscience-stricken whites to clean up the mess in the white middle-class suburbs. I hope we have learned from the Wallace phenomenon that the disease of racism has eaten deeply into the blue-collar urban neighborhoods and mill towns, too. This is another basic reason why the church must be there in strength. And precisely because the missioner speaks from within the blue-collar ethos and out of an "alongsided" stance, he will be heard far more clearly, and will be taken much more seriously, than those who aim their shafts from that alien world "out there" or "up there."

In considering what church resources can be marshaled for knowledgeable and committed reentry of the blue-collar atmosphere, invariably we are predisposed to think in terms of the professional leadership needed. But if a genuine working-class mission is to make an impact, its motor power must come from other quarters. Effective momentum will be brought about by an alert and committed blue-collar laity—by people who have the credentials as long-term co-workers and believers in the blue-collar ethos. These lay men and women can be recognized by their scars, some of which were earned quite recently through their refusal to be swept along with the right-wing mania. It is among them that the new "worker priest" must seek to find a place and to be a presence.

PART III

REVOLUTIONS, VISIONS, AND MIDDLE AMERICA

Two current responses to dehumanization are violence and a mystical quest for personal identity. Neither has taken hold in middle America, but the dynamics of both are intimately related to middle American presence. As detours on the road to rehumanization, they fail to explore the main routes that lie through the politicization of a powerful and equally alienated majority; but they do point us in that direction. In chapter 6 we concentrate on questions of strategy. In chapter 7 we return to the fundamental perspectives discussed in chapter 3, applying them to neomystical experimentation.

THE PIT
AND THE POWER

In the current debate about how to move America toward a more humane society, we need more of two ingredients: a careful reading of the minutes of the previous meetings and an awareness of the processes of power. With apologies to Plato for adapting and revising his figure of the cave, let us explore the "myth of the Pit" as a way of getting some historical perspective and lateral thinking on the questions of violence, nonviolence, reform, and revolution.

The Climb

The recent history of thrust toward social change in this country (preeminently that of and for the black, the young, and the poor, and now enlarging to include other dehumanized groups) follows the pattern of escalation. As minor victories are won, but resistance mounts, one after another method is tried and abandoned. Before we ask how and why it might be otherwise, let us review the characteristic pilgrimage of a liberation movement.

Education

The teachers and preachers have their day early. "Let the putdown lift themselves up. Be wise, be good, and you will make it." Pedagogy and exhortation, however, are for oppressors as well as victims. If we can change their heads and their hearts, things will be different. "Most of all, if the young can be launched with the right kind of nurture we may have a chance with the next generation." So it goes.

Law

Suppose the next generation does come and the slaves are still in chains? Well before that, some begin to ask whether all the books and pamphlets, the dedicated teachers, and fervent preachers are really getting to the root of the matter. At the next stage the source of the problem comes to be seen as less intellectual and spiritual, and more structural. Systematic relationships have to be altered if minds are to be changed. Society's institutions have lost touch with the country's basic charters and must be recalled to them through the courts. The educational system becomes an early candidate, and other structures come under review. The methods of legal pressure replace those of education. A new kind of climbing gear is adopted, not the book but the gavel. A new premise appears; the slave no longer waits for the master to give him his basic rights, but reaches for the justice that is his due.

Politics

As the society is recalled to its basic principles, here and there, the judicial pressures open up new ways toward seeing the sun. But the climber soon discovers that the best laws in the world will not work unless administered fairly. There remains, as well, the question of bad laws. Whether the good laws are implemented or the bad laws get changed depends upon those who execute and legislate. Our pilgrim turns his eyes to the halls of government and concludes he must "throw the rascals out" and put his own people in. His climbing gear must change from the gavel to the ballot. It is on to politics, the mustering of votes to struggle out of the Pit.

Protest

Suppose our people do not get in. As the gentle pressure of politics fails, the climber becomes more demonstrative. The scaler of the heights is still committed to the ethical and political agreements at the root of society, and seeks to appeal to them and to those people of conscience he believes are out there in the community. But now the strategy becomes more forceful. High visibility means public assembly to air grievances: the mass rally, the march, the picket line.

Economic Reprisal

If the appeal to the classic charters, the conscience of the community or oppressor, or public embarrassment of the powers that be fail, then a more direct and sustained attack on the self-interest of the "Establishment" moves into view. It is now the pocketbook and the routines of life that are the targets. They shall be disrupted and the well-being of the foe itself disturbed. The strike, the boycott, the sit-down, and the sit-in are the postures of ascent.

Civil Disobedience

The line is fine between the strike or boycott and civil disobedience. A strike may involve the breach of tyrannical state or national laws, as may also the quiet picket line in a totalitarian town. But now the active intent is to refuse the suzerainty of the dominant powers. Like the demonstrative, this step upward deals in drama—but escalates the level of sacrifice expected of the adherents. Its goal is to awaken whatever conscience there is left in the established order, and more than that, to appeal to the conscience of the neutral masses, to enrage the world looking on, and to ignite the oppressed themselves. There are much more active attempts to subvert the workings of the system, to slow it down, to tie it up. "Go limp, young man, young woman." The social sickness is seen to be so deep that, while the fundamental value system of the society is still honored (for example, by accepting jail penalties), obedience to its present forms is rejected.

Random Violence

If no great change occurs, the momentum up and out now loses the semblance of a "movement" of people and becomes an explosion of fragments against the resisting walls of the Pit. The urge to be free is no longer a tactical effort or planned assault against the enemy, but a rage striking out against the nearest symbol of oppression. And the boundary is crossed from non-violence to violence.

Instrumental Violence: Property

While single acts of random violence may be as destructive as many of those in the category of instrumental violence against property, there is another kind of transition here. Assault is now planned rather than unplanned. It is calculated as instrumental to either short-term goals or long-range revolutionary strategies. Under this rubric are many degrees and distinctions. A crucial one is injury to property or to persons. The former ranges from pouring blood on draft files to major arson and the bombing of buildings. As violence toward property escalates, it is increasingly difficult to avoid hurt to persons as well as property, as has been demonstrated by recent episodes.

Instrumental Violence: Persons

As property symbols of the Establishment become objects of the early expression of violence, so personifications of the power structure are the first natural targets of planned mayhem. Initial tactics include kidnaping of key figures, then assassination, sometimes one related to the other. Next comes guerrilla warfare, defensive on friendly turf, then aggressive on unfriendly, and finally full-scale revolution.

Tripping Out

While the change agents battle to take the heights on one side of the Pit, other gentler pilgrims turn their heads from such affrays and attempt another way out. These ascents may be made by those who have attempted all or part of the other route, and despaired. Now the way up is seen to come by withdrawal rather than confrontation. Its varieties include (1) physical removal from the scene of oppression by migration to a land flowing with milk and honey; and (2) psychic removal from the scene of oppression by chemical, "religious," or other emotional transport to an inner country of felt peace and freedom.

A Colony of Light

For those who find little satisfaction in sorties to never-never lands, inner or outer, a determination to embody the impossible dream in miniature among those of like mind is born. The visionaries get themselves together in communities of intent, either by way of a continuing communal life together or in transient healing groups of encounter. Here is the attempt to catch the rays of the sun in the mirror of a common life along the edges of the abysmal society.

Solo Flight

All the foregoing efforts on both sides of the Pit represent compromises to our final pilgrim. Called for now is a personal heroism that refuses to soil one's hands with the ambiguities of political escalation on the one hand, or withdrawal on the other. There is no opting out intended, but rather the confidence that the individual of moral purity will achieve the goal and inspire others one by one to their own acts of acrobatic courage.

Tunneling

Two conventional assumptions shared by all the travelers are that (1) the effectiveness of the method depends upon the artfulness, commitment, and resources of those who attempt to use it, and (2) the method of change employed is The Method. Options in social change tend to produce ideologies of social change: "Power grows out of the barrel of the gun," "Change the person and you will change the society," and so on. Both these assumptions must be challenged. There is no way to clamber out of the Pit. One can only reach the light by finding it at the end of a tunnel.

There is an opening somewhere along the surface of the Pit's wall, camouflaged by the rock, rubble, and underbrush. The climber has to become an explorer. He must range over the surface of the wall in search of a concealed avenue, a *tunnel of power*. It is the sensitivity to this egress that is lacking in earlier one-dimensional and ideological strategies. Included in the factor of power are the following elements: (1) "The masses." There must be sufficient numbers of people who will either participate directly or indirectly in the movement for change, or at least not impede those who are determined to work for it. These numbers must be, therefore, either a majority or a strong minority with a neutralized or sympathetic majority. (2) Ethos. In tandem with social power must be a psychic readiness in the culture. The grievance or the expectation levels must be sufficiently high, or the conscience or value premises of the society sufficiently prepared. (3) A core of change agents. They must have the kind of discipline, depth of commitment, and organizational expertise to harness the readied cultural vitalities. (4) Technology. Access to significant techniques that form the mind and structures of the society must be possible. One of the new factors operative today is the availability of these resources, as evidenced by things as disparate as the offset press that makes possible an underground newspaper and Herman Kahn's forecasts of accessibility to miniature nuclear weaponry by paramilitary groups. (5) Charismatic leadership. Whether history produces a Martin Luther King, Jr., or a Kenneth Kaunda, or these prophetic figures produce the history, they are part and parcel of any modern liberation struggle.

The search for the power tunnel, or network of tunnels, will entail three insights gained from the first unsuccessful efforts to scale the wall. One of these is the need for lateral thinking and innovation at whatever level attempted. We must retrace the steps of our pilgrimage with a new set of implements—tools to dig with rather than to hike with. Take education as an example. If traditional formalistic methods do not work, the exploration of new directions might point to guerrilla theater, the human-potential movement, free schools, a citizen's press, new use of computers "to relate people to people and people to ideas" (Theobald), contextual education, and "pedagogy of the oppressed."

Another point of special concentration, if not fresh strategy, is the development of parallel structures and counterinstitutions. The purpose of these is, on one hand, to elude the captivity attendant to reformist efforts in conventional institutions and, on the other, to give participatory dignity and a support system to the aggrieved and thus raise their consciousness and power. The black community is now actively engaged in this kind of strategy. It is also at work in new political configurations alongside the standard political parties, women's liberation movements, community organization, new media, and communitarian experiments that run from religion through law to revolution. (The various communitarian experiments differ from the cultural commune in their direct engagement in the processes of social change.)

A third new guideline is the reassessment of the vulnerability of those places of ascent that seemed most perilous on the first climb. The tunnel crust may be thinnest precisely where the heights at first appeared most unassailable. For example, the resistance to the upward mobility of the black, the young, and the poor by middle America is a sign of deep-seated frustration with its own lot. The flag waved so angrily at the change agents of the sixties is less a call to arms against minority groups and more a distress signal run up by "forgotten Americans" calling attention to their own dehumanization. Blue-collar and white-collar suburbanites suffer many of the same physical and psychic disabilities that a technocratic society lays upon its more vocal minorities. Ravages run from urban chaos, through consumer peril and medical breakdown, to job insecurity and the sacrifice of its young in a futile war. And extending through all the more visible injustices is the same powerlessness of the blue-white communities that is experienced by the black, brown, and red. The social power necessary for freeing all the victims of the Pit lies in these kinds of multitudes entombed in the tunnel itself. The frustration of middle America has to be redirected away from its fellow victims and toward the technocratic structures and elites. To that end, movement for social justice will work toward rainbow coalitions that enlist all the dehumanized —and in so doing tap the sources of social power that can effect fundamental change.

The Range of Exploration

Where do we make our probes for the tunnel opening? That decision is illuminated by a vision and some givens, things unseen and things seen.

The vision has to do with the fundamental orientation of the change agent. If those committed to social change are lured by the dream of a fully human reconciled society, a vision of shalom, then strategies must begin at "zero alienation." Such efforts allow the greatest maneuvering room for reconciliation, attempt to avoid destructive forms of confrontation, and disavow violence. To begin again is to begin, therefore, at the ground-zero and near-ground-zero levels of education, law, and politics.

Already, however, we have proposed different kinds of education, law, and politics, which take into account the givens of Establishment resistance that impede the original pilgrimage. While lured and judged by the vision of reconciliation, efforts in range of zero alienation work with parallel structures that presuppose estrangement and anticipate conflict, and thus they must be prepared to escalate, possibly to the point of massive civil disobedience.

There is another given that is related to the particular line of violence-nonviolence so central to contemporary debates on strategy. That given is the middle American constituency that holds decisive swing power. Middle Americans enlist in movements for creative social change that use tactics up to and including civil disobedience (for example, postal and air traffic control "strikes"). But beyond that point all recent evidence seems to suggest only counterproductivity. Where there has been any flirtation with violence by forgotten Americans it has been in support of the status quo, or even the status quo ante. In our current ethos (although this was not so as recently as the labor organizing violence of the thirties) there seems to be an unquestioned assumption that in middle America violence is the prerogative of the state in international and domestic matters, so that even its extralegal use by middle Americans tends to support the way things are now. We've come a long way from Minutemen of the 1770's to those of the 1970's. Revolutions attempted in a North American context whose silent center guards the entrance to the power tunnel can only produce an explosion whose debris will again cover over the exit.

If our soundings are correct about the location of the aperture, it must also be said that there is a supportive function served by activity on the margins of the opening. Even those who labor up the other side, taking the ways of withdrawal, serve an ancillary purpose. Their judgment upon the way things are cannot be overlooked by the society, especially because some of the most attractive children of that society may be so involved. Further, the economic and social loss to the country also takes its toll in these forms of absenteeism. Meanwhile, at the other end of the spectrum, the threat of violence may also contribute to the attractiveness of the movements for nonviolent change. As the revolutions of Gandhi and King were found to be more palatable than the designs of extremists waiting in the wings, so comparable thrusts which range from education to civil disobedience may in the seventies receive unintended support from the threats of the adventurist.

A Concluding Observation

Much commentary from the religious community on the questions of social change is similar to popular secular analyses; both deal in heavy ideology. From the "theology of revolution" to the "nonviolent cross," it is assumed that faith has its obvious methodologies. In the foregoing reflections there are, indeed, theological assumptions that provide the orientation points: liberation and reconciliation as controlling visions of the kingdom of God, sin and finitude as realities with which visionaries have to come to terms in translating ultimate hopes into penultimate strategies. But there are no clear programmatic derivatives from these reference points. We have therefore sought to deideologize the Christian contribution to the dialogue by putting the perceptions of vision and reality through the filter of recent historical experience, and looking for new options that appear out of this transaction. That kind of lateral thinking might transform the quest for freedom from the Pit from a futile exercise in mountain climbing into a productive effort in tunneling.

Chapter 7
AQUARIAN DREAMS
AND EARTHED HOPES

While bombs were being planted in campus research centers last fall, University of Hawaii students witnessed another kind of confrontation. A graffiti war was in progress at a central construction site. One week the fences read, "Come Sunday night to 1212 University Avenue. Psychic sleep, natural high. Hare Krishna, Hare Krishna, Krishna Krishna, Hare Hare, Hare Rama. . . ." The next week the mantras disappeared and in their place appeared, "Jesus loves you. Flee hell, find heaven. Turn on with Christ, 20th and Pahoa Avenue, 7:15 P.M., Mondays." Moreover, the attacking "Jesus freaks" announced they were going to carry the battle to the streets of Waikiki. There, in front of the International Market Place, the chanting Krishnites would be lovingly enveloped by the sounds and sights of "Onward, Christian Soldiers."

Are all these religious goings-on native only to our exotic mid-Pacific island? Not so, to judge from the popularity of such songs as "My Sweet Lord" (with the juxtaposition, interestingly, of the Hare Krishna refrain with a Jesus lullaby). Or think about the paperback store shelves bulging with Krishnamurti's books, the Who's Peter Townshend fervently testifying to Meher Baba in a recent issue of *Rolling Stone*, the revival of interest in the Maharishi. And, of course, there is the flirtation with ESP, I Ching, tarot cards, astrology, witchcraft, and a host of new practitioners of the now establishment Zen.

How do these religious impulses relate to the Christian faith, and how does the Christian community relate to them? Honolulu is a hospitable laboratory for such inquiries. Teaching at the university, where seventeen hundred students each semester crowded into the religion courses, and serving on the staff of the remarkable Crossroads church that gave sanctuary recently to a commune of local Krishnites ousted from various former "temples" by annoyed neighbors (the previous year Crossroads gave sanctuary to forty GI's protesting the Vietnam War) made for a rich learning experience in the ways of neomysticism.

Whether they read it in the books of some currently popular diagnostician (Theodore Roszak, *The Making of a Counter Culture,* Charles Reich, *The Greening of America,* and others) or come to it as the result of a hassle at a peace demonstration, a pot party bust, or involvement in an ecological crusade, there is a common picture developing in the minds of the arriving generation of middle-class young. They look out on a society framed by its picture tubes, high rises, and jet streams. In that scene all modern technology, from lasers to miniature circuitry, conspire to revolutionize the worlds of work and play. Back of the products lie the premises: the methods of the laboratory and the shop floor—empirical, rational, pragmatic—define the limits of reality, prescribe the right way to deal with it, and promise a horn of plenty. Further, way up there somewhere at the controls of these awesome instruments seem to be cadres of "experts" with their own plans and plots. Sometimes this high scheming appears to be done in such compartmentalized fashion that it looks like "nobody is in charge."

And what have these gods wrought? Plague, pestilence, famine, and death. The divine promises of technocracy have not been kept; instead of fulfillment has come the apocalypse of pollution, hunger, hate, and war.

If the science-technology of the West has brought us to a dead end, then it's time to look for another way out, so the scenario reads. Go East, young human. Those who tread this new path will not tinker with the outer world but will discover and relate to the inner cosmos; not seek to subdue and control everything but groove with the All; not ratiocinate and dissect, but experience and feel; not talk, talk, talk, or act, act, act, but meditate and contemplate; not revel in things man-made and urban, but learn to love things natural and close to the soil; not be attracted to the complexity, hardness, and precision of the technician, but to the simplicity, softness, and gentleness of the guru; not live by the creed that it's every man for himself and the devil take the hindmost, but believe in human goodness, risk the act of sharing, and affirm things communal; not adopt the rigid manners and morals of middle America, but be "freed up" in lifestyle, from hair and clothing to music and mating. The birth of the "new religions" (the title of Jacob Needleman's recent work on neomysticism) of feeling, fantasy, mystery, and communality is a natural expression of the new quest.

One other stream feeding into the romantic reaction to technocracy and its failures, reinforcing particularly the mystical aspects, is the personal struggle to assess the relation of chemical stimulation of the brain to our perception of reality. Sometime psychedelic drugs are used as a part of religious rituals. More often, devotees declare that they no longer require artificial stimuli, for a "natural high" is available to them through their newfound rites. The attempt to grasp and manipulate the physiological routes of enlightenment has recently led to the final irony: the invention of the alphaphone, a technological device that facilitates the production of brain waves associated with some kinds of religious experience. In any case, a certain love-hate relationship with a chemistry that promises better things for better living contributes to the neomystical fevers.

Another East

There were several conceptual guidelines that proved helpful in the Honolulu laboratory. Of course, they presuppose human relationships by churchmen to these constituencies (relationships yet largely absent), such as presence in and dialogue with the neomystic and advocacy for their communities when under harassment. Putting aside the Jesus people for the moment, let us concentrate on the varieties of "Eastern religion" that dominate the current religious scene. (*Christ Is Dead—Buddha Lives!*, incidentally, is the subtitle of John Garabedian and Orde Coombs's study of the phenomenon, *Eastern Religions in the Electric Age*.)

Worth mentioning first is a rather obvious but almost universally ignored fact: Christianity is also an Eastern religion. So is Judaism. As such, they are sensitive to the dimensions of mystery and unity that draw the counterculture to other Eastern options. Eastern Orthodox explore the mystical depths, Francis of Assisi celebrates the living earth of the ecologists, and communitarian experiments abound in Christian history. Counterparts to all are found in Judaism. Western Christianity, in which these perceptions are buried, has so accommodated to its technocratic setting that it is difficult for the young to see these riches. But they are there.

However, they are there with a difference. The spirituality growing out of the Judeo-Christian stream struggles toward contemplation that is a companion to action and talk, rather than the antithesis of them. The Presence is sought in the midst of social and political ferment. In our own times the heirs of the perspective set their faces against the same technocracy and rationalism rejected by the counterculture, but refuse the antitechnological and anti-intellectual mold in which the protest is cast.

The style difference is traceable to a perspectival source: one oriental religious tradition broke step with its sisters. Jews and Christians do not move toward, nor are they moved by, what Arend Th. van Leeuwen calls the "basic apperception" that underlies the religion of their Eastern kin, an intuition that he believes may be dormant in all of us. This feel for "the way things are" emphasizes the essential unity of all things that exists behind, and is more fundamental than, the diversities and alienations that daily assault us. Religions that cultivate this apperception testify to the illusoriness of the self and the passingness of history, seek to slow time down for unseeking contemplation of "the abiding present" (Alan Watts), and strive for fusion with the All. Cultural fruits of this orientation include the encouragement of an "ontocratic pattern" in which political hierarchies, with their attendant caste structures, are the executors of a cosmic logic. The new Aquarians lodge their protest against technocracy and express their longing for unity in these kinds of religious sensibilities. But their apolitical life-style leaves unchallenged the castes and hierarchies accredited by the gods of our secular society.

It is tempting to speculate about interrelationships of Aquarian drug experience (immersion in "the private sea"), the religious trip that invites absorption of the droplet of self in the sea of reality (see Thomas Braden's *The Private Sea* and *The Age of Aquarius*), and the fundamental apperception. Do drugs and religion "develop" the apperception like a film in solution? Do Freud's comments on religion as "oceanic feeling" shed any light on the connections? We leave such questions open-ended, being concerned here to suggest how neomysticism may be part of a wider religious phenomenon that takes its cues from a direction very different from that of one small stubborn Near Eastern tribe.

The singularity of Israel lay in its orientation point for mystery and unity: not in and down, but out and ahead. It took its bearings from events in its history and saw these happenings as disclosure situations of a promised reality. It was not mesmerized by a stationary light shining from the depths and suffusing our environs, but kept its eye upon a pillar of fire up front that lured its people out of the past, through the present, toward a Not Yet. The Christian community took up this future-oriented covenant, seeing Bethlehem, Galilee, Golgotha, Easter, and Pentecost in continuity with the exodus. And the New Israel believed, and believes, that the rays of the ever-receding horizon light have been caught in the mirror of these Jesus events.

What one does in the light of this lure of futurity is different from the course taken by the neomystic, who seeks to penetrate the veil of the temporal Now by an interior descent into the divine effulgence. On one hand, there is an abiding curiosity about certain past temporalities because these events are apertures into the future. There is also a zeal to tell and celebrate the revelatory tales. On the other hand, the vision of how the world could be, and will be, is so different from the way it is now that the visionary cannot be servile before the givens, inner or outer. He is goaded to rearrange and bend them into signposts toward the future.

Let us focus in more closely on two aspects of this eschatological style, relationships to nature and history. In doing it we shall also look more particularly at some of the characteristics of the biblical vision.

Nature

The great dream of fulfillment is one of shalom. The soil and the sea, the plants and the animals are all part of that final hope for wholeness, unity, peace. Rich biblical metaphors point to the healing of a crippled creation. The foretaste of, and mandate toward, that end are found in the one who stills the tempest and overcomes the final wound of physical things in his resurrection. Moreover, he furnishes us with a new pair of eyes to see in nature the healing rhythms already at work, to see in the birds of the air and the flowers of the field, evidence of an aborning shalom.

To one community within the realm of nature comes a special charge to build the earth toward that vision. Rooted in all the contingencies of the natural world, yet gifted as well with a power to imagine and act upon fresh scenarios, the human race is called to coresponsibility with the Builder. The project is harassed on every side: fitful labor and absenteeism by the craftsmen; their inclination to throw up Babels whose weight fractures the earth and whose collapse scatters the work teams; the failures of the materials themselves, nature's own internal breakdowns. But creation and re-creation go on apace with signs of hope left by their Source in the works of nature and man.

That kind of perspective begets affirmations and warnings. Science-technology, as humanity's most recent expression of its capacity to understand the workings of its world and the freedom to ennoble it, becomes a potential ally in the call to build the earth. With the readiness to use this awesome instrument come some sobering sister commitments: (1) awareness of the temptations to abuse the power that human ingenuity has given us; (2) sensitivity to the delicate textures of healing that are already in nature, in the company of which the work of building will have to go on; and (3) loyalty to the final vision of shalom by which all the technological blueprints must be measured.

There is here no romanticizing of nature or invitation to melt into it. Nature is short of its goal and broken in the pursuit of it. But it is not evil or illusory. While not God, it is good, a piece of the final dream and a partner in the journey toward new creation. Humanity is to honor the traces of the future there and be an active agent of their upbuilding.

History

The same action toward the future is to be found in our dealings with history. The new heavens and new earth house a New Jerusalem. This picture of a new society on the screen of tomorrow lures us away from the present and makes impossible any sacral confirmation of the way things are. There is no ontocratic pattern in which hierarchical social structures are viewed as the exteriorization of cosmic reality. Nor is there any guarantee of an Eternal Now that can be reached by passage through, or descent below, this withoutness. Society's patterns are human, not divine, a product of that part of creation freed to make its own way toward a temporarily distanced vision. The sacred is not a fait accompli, but a task to be done and a promise to be kept. Historical action is charged to call into question all structures that militate against that Not Yet, and build new ones that chase the dream.

While history is littered with shattered dreams, it is not one vast trash can. Contrary to simplistic futurism, the time before the end is not God-forsaken. The Absolute Future appears not only in Christ, but also, fleetingly, wherever glimmers of shalom are to be seen. This kind of Nowness is the ground of hope. But more, it gives direction to the inwardness appropriate to future-oriented faith. Devotion is through a glass darkly, eschatologically modest, communion not union, sacramental not sacral. And the sacramental happens, as did the first sacrament, in the moil and toil of things. All this is a long way from the mystical and neomystical quest for healing in the waters in the womb.

The Jesus People

Where do the "Jesus freaks" fit in to this analysis? They are both more and less than their professed identity.

The conventional fundamentalist who courts the young Jesus people and claims them as notches on his evangelistic guns may be in for a surprise. While their vocabulary resembles that of a very conservative Christianity, the timing of their appearance on the religious scene, their counterculture garb and hair style, and sometimes their communal life-style hint that we have to do with something more than restorationism. These factors suggest that they are part of the same revolt against the society of their elders as are the self-consciously oriental varieties of religious experience. The Jesus people have seized upon more readily accessible symbols to express their Consciousness III sensibilities. (Is this strategically wiser than those who reach for the bizarre, or does it suggest a more domesticated rebellion? The signs point to the latter. While the Krishnites dominated the religious street scene in cosmopolitan Honolulu, the Jesus freaks were drawing hundreds of teen-agers to meetings in Kailua, a largely middle-class white suburb.) What effect this will have ultimately on the Consciousness I and II mentalities of the conservative Christianity that currently harbors them should make an interesting story.

From our angle of vision, the Jesus freaks are also, sadly, less than their Christian identity implies. To date there is little evidence of their commitment to an event-grounded—and future-oriented—faith. The new pietism nestles as comfortably into oppressive political and economic systems as any other neomysticism. Judging from the life-style of its proponents, turning on with Jesus means dropping out of the social struggle. A Christ so easily domesticated in the present and imprisoned in interiority is hardly recognizable. Neither is one who encourages uncritical acceptance of biblical literalism, religious fantasy, and the abdication of the intellectual quest. In both its strong and weak points, therefore—as a critic of technocracy and in the alternatives it offers to it—the "Jesus trip" appears to be more a product of the counterculture than an authentic recovery of the powerful symbols of the Christian faith.

The other popular Jesus cult, devotion associated with the rock opera *Jesus Christ Superstar,* is also both more and less than its label might suggest. Along with the rest of the counterculture, the music launches an attack on the sentimentalities of the Establishment, in this case, particularly the conventional wisdom about an unworldly Jesus. When it rejects the docetism of popular religion and underscores the humanity of Jesus, the opera is more orthodox than it realizes. In fact, it should shame all of us in the church for being so long a party to the anemic caricature of an enfleshed God. But its rendition of Jesus as a superstar in the current antihero tradition is such an echo of current assumptions by Aquarians that the radical over-against-ness of Jesus is censored and the gospel thoroughly tamed. Like most of the biographies of Christ, *Jesus Christ Superstar* is autobiography. As such it is incapable of doing the critical and revolutionary work a characterization of Christ must do to be faithful to the God who refuses to be made over in our image.

Relationships
of Christian Community
and the New Religions

Out of the theological sorting come some guidelines for relating to the concerns of practitioners of neomysticism.

1. Behind and through the often strange religious idiom, profound human insights and astute social criticism are to be found. Neomysticism exposes gaping holes in our society. Its rituals and fantasies are cries from those wounded by technocratic machinery. On the other hand, its reveries and disciplines point to how the world could be if another cultural course were to be taken. The communitarian experiments undertaken in light of the new visions should disturb us and call us toward new social forms and life-styles. Beyond being symptoms and signs, new religious patterns may also be ways of coping. Why should not *Yoga over Forty* lead to new self-understanding and health for middle-aged Christians? Further, human tenderness and ecological sensitivity are in short supply in a technocratic era, and are to be applauded for what they are even when in exotic garb. Again, contemplation and meditation are valuable ways of centering down in our chaotic and harried daily routines. These are all secular insights into the ways of healing and dream of wholeness. Let us, then, secularize them. Honor them for their value by detaching them from the religious paraphernalia and using them in the service of shalom.

2. There are more specifically religious, as well as ethical, resonances in neomysticism to the Christian faith. The refusal to accept the visibilities as definitive of reality is surely one of them. The love of God for his own sake is another. The pressures of a pragmatic and secular time have tried mightily to program out these intimations of transcendence. We can be grateful to the protestation of the neomystic for making us more alert to this captivity. Perhaps we must do some much more serious digging in our own mystical traditions—from the Eastern churches to the Western mystics—for these latter groupings build their window into reality with the ageric and futuric tools of the biblical tradition.

3. The popular slogan of the sixties calling for a "morato-

rium on God talk" ought to be reexamined. We must take another look at the kerygmatic dimension of the church's mission. This certainly does not mean a return to the shouting evangelist. Faithfulness to the urgent secular claims of our time means that the tale can only be told in the context of real deeds, and not much above the whisper appropriate to physicians caught up in the healing of hurts. But for humans whose wounds are not only physical, and whose thirst is for mystery and meaning, other options from the East must find their place alongside those of the swami and guru.

Aquarians
and Middle Americans

The foregoing reflections on the religious hungers of the counterculture seem to have little bearing on middle America. Indeed, they were not written with the latter in mind. However, these thoughts are included here because of very important implicit relationships between these two seemingly disparate groups.

As noted briefly in chapter 3, there is an intriguing overlap in astrological interest by draft-age youth and mill-town housewife. Beyond that, the general neomystical trends in the counterculture and the strength of pietism in middle America (ranging from the continuing appeal of the mass revival, through the followings of radio evangelists, to the growing pockets of pentecostal practice) indicate striking similarities. What is common to all these tendencies is an understanding of religion essentially as a turning "in and down." The self faces inward to contemplate its own ambiguities and seek respite from them, or meditate upon its possibilities and exfoliate them. Others are beckoned by the convert into the same depths to rearrange their destinies, find God in their hearts, or serenity for their souls.

An inwardness that does not make its way back into the hurly-burly arena of the common life with the marching orders of liberation is more a symptom of the cultural crisis than a solution. But symptoms are not to be scorned, for they do tell us about the state of the body politic. Neomysticism and pietism are warning signals in the fever zones of the young and the unyoung. Both of the latter suffer the disease of dehumanization.

Both experience erosion of their lives. Their moan of pain is heard and seen in the rising religious temperatures within their subcultures.

A further symptom of demoralization is the assumption of powerlessness that is common to neomystic and pietist. The controls over the future are in the hands of a Force or forces which expect only our submission. We are called to align ourselves dutifully to the cosmic givens. This is more an autobiographical report by young and unyoung of the sense of helplessness before the technocratic juggernaut than the biography of a God who empowers men to shape their own future.[1] Neomysticism and pietism accredit the captivity of their proponents and abort the liberation instincts of high religion.

But there are clues for health as well as signs of sickness in the religious quest of both Aquarian and middle American. A world free of war, hate, and hurt is a theme common to the inwardly reified visions of the neomystic and the pietist. They do dream about liberation and shalom. But these remain alienated dreams as long as the route to them leads into a cavernous interiority. Marx wanted to "stand Hegel on his head" in order to overcome the estrangement of philosophical ideas from revolutionary practice; here we find it more meaningful to turn religious ideas inside out—and ahead.

The religious stirrings found among the Aquarian and the middle American are yet one more bit of evidence of a shared plight. And if religious introversion can be extroverted, they are one more reason for working toward that unlikely coalition of the barbered and the bearded whose alliance can turn captivity to liberation.

PART IV

LIBERATION MODELS

Are there any signs of liberation in middle America? Of course there are. In this last section we are particularly interested in evidence of grass-roots struggle with dehumanization. We look, also, for liberation momentum that brings together coalitions of young, black, and poor with unyoung, unblack, and unpoor—the tunnel out of "the Pit." The two models discussed, developed in the heart of middle America, did make allies of minority groups and many middle Americans, but also angered others in both camps. The excitement and pain of each were very much part of my life and that of my family for half a decade. Besides describing their genesis, I have tried to identify the factors that made for survival and the achievement of their goals. Both the newspaper and desegregation of the city schools, incidentally, are very much part of the community's life today.

To achieve small victories in liberation here and there, it takes liberated people. I speak in the last chapter of middle Americans who have cast off the chains of fear and flight that yet bind so many in the silent center. I dub them "mid-libs." May their tribe increase!

Chapter 8
VOICE OF
THE VOICELESS

Would you believe—a town in which all three newspapers, the TV station, and a radio station are owned by the same family, where the news and views of the powerful get full airing and those of the powerless get short shrift?

Would you believe—a town in which the young, the black, the poor, the professor, the poverty worker, the church-in-world Christian and Jew banded together to publish their own newspaper, where the powerless took it into their own hands to "give voice to voiceless views—to print the unprinted news"?

The first is not hard to imagine. Indeed, 90 percent of America's communities have a monopoly press. The second is difficult to swallow, but it is beginning to happen. We tell the story of one "irresponsible weekly" in the small city of Lancaster, Pennsylvania, where the news monolith described in the first paragraph reigned until the birth of LIP, the *Lancaster Independent Press*. Its experience may be of some value as a laboratory for others planning their RIP's, PIP's, or NIP's.

Challenge and Response

Lancastrians read their newspaper as faithfully as their Bibles, and treat the former as "gospel" like the latter. A loose coalition of the community's powerless discovered this in the peace, poverty, and civil-rights ferment of the decade in this Pennsylvania Dutch metropolitan community of 300,000. Often the editorial and the "news" stories were as unbalanced and destructive in these areas as the letters to the editor from the noisy right wing.

The press gave their benediction to the status quo, with one important exception: the editor of the morning daily regularly took strong stands in favor of civil-rights concerns, locally and nationally. Shortly after several courageous editorials supported a plan to desegregate the city's junior high schools in the face of the fury of a thousand petitioners from the white neighborhoods affected, a strange reshuffling took place in the editorial staff. A new name appeared on the masthead as managing editor —a former staff member of the evening paper—and the word was out that the regular editor had been relieved of effective control of the paper. From that point on, the "liberal" noises that had been made were silenced.

In the overheated months of 1968, stories in all papers appeared with increasing frequency about beatings, "riots," and shootings in which black militants appeared to be the culprits. Nothing was said about white motorcycle gangs that rode through the ghetto taunting black youths; nor was background given on known instances of white provocation; nor were the many grievances against police tactics in the black community aired. Local peace activists received particularly rough treatment in the news media. Caricatures of the student revolution and the new breed of high school youth were plentiful. The Community Action Program came under regular criticism.

Responsible coverage reached a new low in the fall of 1968, when several young, black militants were arrested for the murder of a white pedestrian; the defense attorney pled for a change of venue, using piles of news clippings which he rightly claimed had contributed to the inflaming of community passions. It appeared that it would be a repeat performance of the situation described in *Murder in Paradise,* the book reporting the strange Lancaster trial of a Franklin and Marshall College student who was executed in the 1950's for the murder of a local citizen. At that trial, the defense attorney also pled, without success, for a change of venue on the grounds of an inflammatory press. The black youths were more fortunate. Halfway through the trial, a visiting judge threw the case out of court because there was insufficient evidence to warrant continuing the prosecution.

During this period, talk about the press among civil-rights leaders and churchmen took an increasingly serious turn. Restlessness with the situation led three clergymen—George Geisler of Trinity United Church of Christ, East Petersburg, former chairman of the Social Action Committee of the Lancaster Council of Churches; Allen Kroehler, director of the Lancaster Theological Seminary's Laboratory for Leadership and Learning; and me—to pay a visit to the editor of one of the country's leading crusading small papers: the nearby York (Pa.) *Gazette & Daily.* Awed by the thought of starting from scratch, we thought the best that could be managed was a Lancaster edition of the York paper. However, similar overtures from Baltimore, Harrisburg, and Gettysburg had proved unproductive, and the editor advised us to launch our own.

After making some soundings among old allies in the National Association for the Advancement of Colored People, the American Civil Liberties Union, the peace movement, church leadership, potential new allies in the remnants of the McCarthy organization, the editor of the renewal center Encounter's newsletter (which served as a kind of clearinghouse for information about community action), and CAP participants, an organizing meeting was called at the Laboratory for Leadership and Learning. Allen Kroehler's minutes read: "Twenty-four citizens of Lancaster County met September 18, 1968, to consider the need for more responsible news coverage. It was agreed that the need was urgent." Four task forces were formed to deal with purpose, layout, distribution, and fund-raising. Then began five months of daydreaming, brainstorming, wrangling, sifting, retreat and advance.

With the odd assortment of people that gathered around this venture—almost totally lacking in journalistic experience—the gestation of LIP was something to behold. Clergymen found themselves training to be reporters, a seminary professor's wife became coordinator of photography, an RCA engineer became chief solicitor of funds, a housewife tried her hand at a TV column, an advertising executive took responsibility for making up crossword puzzles, an anthropologist took over distribution, and a history professor agreed to become the editor. Meanwhile, a dedicated but nervous attorney plotted the course through the anticipated legal and libel shoals.

There were also some professionals in this strange mix. A former editor of a local paper, now retired, met with us about technical matters, explaining along the way how he had put ventures like ours out of business. Another editor, from out of town, met with the planning committee to describe the hurdles in great detail and to advise us to quit before it was too late. Another counseled us that it was impossible to start without at least $500,000 on hand. A national communications executive advised us to have a radio program instead.

Friends came and went in the five months of organizing. Some

who were interested in the effort because of the chance for newspaper experience beat a hasty retreat when they discovered
LIP's controversial bent. Members of the Students for a Democratic Society appeared inquisitive at first, but soon concluded
that nothing much could happen with a lot of middle-class,
churchy types. Several of our early black-militant supporters
were jailed. Some CAP personnel disappeared after meditation
on the Hatch Act. An educational television station recorded a
meeting with a view toward doing a documentary, but retired
after deciding that the LIP venture was an improbable one. Sur-
vivors stumbled ahead.

By the first of the year, certain tangible signs appeared. The
group agreed on a name and designed an appropriate logo—the
letters LIP with an intertwined interrobang—that found its way
into a six-foot banner and some newly printed stationery. The
banner fluttered one Saturday over a workshop in Lancaster's
oldest church building, Trinity Lutheran Church, in which sev-
enty-five volunteers participated, sorting themselves into perma-
nent committees and task forces for projected issues. A new
headquarters was found—Encounter's three-story downtown
building—after a seminary administration, anxious about the
tax status of its Laboratory for Leadership and Learning building, asked LIP to move. A card was printed to solicit funds,
with such optimistic categories as $500 for patron membership
and $1,000 for life membership. The group acquired a treasurer,
bonded him, and deposited its $234 in a newly established ac-
count.

Most important, the group finally decided who it was. The
statement of purpose filed in the incorporation proceedings announced:

The Lancaster Independent Press is a non-profit weekly newspaper published
by Lancaster citizens for Lancaster citizens. Its purposes are to: (1) Publish
news of local and national affairs that is not available to the average Lancaster reader—to print the unprinted news. (2) Provide a forum for opinion
that is denied a public hearing—to give a voice to voiceless views. LIP affirms
the words, Some men see things as they are and say, why? I dream of things
that never were and say, why not?

While this statement offers a broad secular platform for all
who are struggling for a more just and humane community,
those of us who came to LIP because of our Christian commitments read it with lenses formed from those Christian convic-

tions. Thus, it speaks in Christian futurity idiom of a shalom in which all sorts and conditions of men will have a chance to participate meaningfully, echoing Martin Luther King, Jr.'s dream of a society reconciled. It affirms the dignity of the "weak things of the world and despised" and seeks to be an instrument of the God who "casts the mighty from their seats and exalts those of low degree." It applies the biblical realism about the corruptibility of absolute power to a monopoly media, and seeks to disperse it.

Walking on Water

With its dreams and its $234, LIP moved into Encounter's downtown quarters. Borrowed typewriters, filing cabinets, chairs, and tables began to appear, along with some very talented people eager to help where they could. Among that number were a group of VISTA workers who promptly filled the positions of city editor, assistant cartoonist, and, as we were soon to discover, adventurous reporters. The spacious third-floor "editorial offices" even began to look like a newspaper stereotype, complete with stagnant coffee cups, litter, and a chain-smoking editor.

In the first week of March 1969 seven thousand copies of LIP hit the streets of Lancaster. Of these, two thousand were bulk orders to some forty churches that had been convinced by an articulate clergyman that it was the kind of thing that renewal-oriented congregations should boost. Many were hawked for 10 cents a copy on the downtown streets, in suburban shopping centers, or sold door to door by the children of some of the organizers and by college students. Others were distributed outside area high schools by the cub reporters who had helped to form the first issue on the subject of youth. An additional fourteen hundred were sent as free samples to a list of potential sympathizers, and the rest were distributed from Hawaii to Maine in a quest for outside support.

The excitement over the sheer "happenedness" of the paper tended to obscure, at first, some hard facts about its quality. Soon enough, our well-wishers and others pointed out that there was hardly any news in the first issue except a scoop picture of a steeple cross being placed on a local church. Also, for a paper that purported to be crusading, the posture seemed generally rather timid. There were, however, some in-depth articles on the youth of the black community, excerpts from the ACLU statement on civil rights for students, a story about high school underground newspapers in the country, a calendar of events, a cartoon strip, and other items. The most popular feature seemed to be the centerfold poster with a striking picture of two smiling "flower children" on a park wall hovering over a sedate, middle-aged couple on a bench below, with the signatures of many of the LIP workers and appropriate graffiti surrounding it.

The quality and bite of the paper took a marked turn upward in succeeding issues, thanks to improved organization and feedback, and the coming of a free-lance editor and his wife, Lamar and Sally Hoover. A second issue on the housing theme had some hard-hitting commentary and data on slumlords, a story of discontent among both white and black poor over housing conditions, church involvement in housing efforts, a Puerto Rican column, and even two ads. The third issue, on peace, marked the expansion of the paper from eight to twelve pages, with such items as the story of Lancaster as the conscientious objector capital of the state because of the presence of several peace denominations, the personnel and operations of the local Selective Service System, and the growing militancy of the peace movement.

The publication of unprinted news took on dramatic reality with a front-page story of a respected school-board member who had been purged from the fall Republican slate because of his courageous vote several years previously in favor of the integration of the junior high schools—a tale which has yet to appear in any of the conventional media. In a similar vein were interviews with the black attorney who defended the youths released from the murder trial for lack of evidence and a local peace protestor (the case against him—for returning business reply cards with "Stop the war" on them—had also been dropped). To the Puerto Rican column was added one in Greek (as the LIP offset printing process enabled it to photograph Father Alexander Veronis' Greek typescript letters, the word to the established media since has been, Can you top this?) The first comic strip was joined by a second, and now there were five ads.

Succeeding issues on such themes as local government and area higher education ran studies of minority parties (Democratic and American Independent), an interview with a Birch Society leader and a black militant (both granted exclusively to LIP because it was not part of the "Establishment press"), a column by high school students, reports of activities in the Jewish community, reports of student and faculty ferment in area colleges, and notes on local educational TV.

During the first year LIP scored a number of scoops on events that the local papers steered clear of: local peace moratorium activity and Lancaster citizenry's participation in national protest action, inside reporting on student ferment in both local high schools and colleges, outspoken essays on women's liberation, sprightly commentary and coverage on the local ecological crusade, tenant opinion on an overbearing housing authority, and sensitive black poetry from behind prison walls. In a nice piece of historical irony, LIP acquired as a regular feature writer the author Richard Gehman, whose incisive pen now continues to probe the community he had written about years before in *Murder in Paradise*.

On its first anniversary LIP achieved its goal of going from biweekly to weekly. With a modest but reliable clientele of advertisers, five hundred regular subscribers, a minimum regular press run of twenty-five hundred copies, and both local and national boosters, it displayed both a past and future that awed even its most hopeful founders.

LIP Draws Blood

When the names of LIP incorporators were published in the legal notices of the dailies in January 1969, the city accepted the news with its customary Pennsylvania Dutch reserve. Apart from our attorney's receiving some good-natured joshing on lawyer's row, and several nasty letters expressing ire over the latest hobbyhorse of the town's "radicals" (the group of incorporators included the president of the NAACP, an ACLU leader, a college professor, a businesswoman with a record of ardent civil-rights activity, and a seminary professor), reaction was not discernible. After the initial issues, however, that picture changed.

LIP's research of racist pressure that prompted the dropping of the school-board member earned the wrath of the local Republican machine. It evoked the same reaction from the Democratic Establishment when it probed for bias and opportunism in the sidetracking of scattered-site housing plans and the treatment of welfare recipients. Interviews with the black militants and their lawyer which aired stinging criticism of county judicial procedures, jail conditions, and police practices made few friends in those precincts.

For some, the sheer existence of LIP, quite apart from what it said, raised blood pressures. The response of one woman at a church gathering where LIP was invited to explain its goal was not atypical. "How dare you!" she demanded. Indeed, to cast suspicion on the performance of the established press by starting a new paper is more than some elements of the Lancaster community can take. As the former president of one of the area's major industries put it, "It's subversive!"

Mild harassment followed the rhetoric. Our first printer strangely withdrew his services the day the first copy was scheduled for the press. Our present printer, whose courage and commitments have led him to be our technical adviser as well, had certain trade privileges taken away the week he joined us. The proprietor of a drugstore, livid with rage after the third issue, ejected our professorial distributor and his bundle of fourth-issue copies. Organizers and editorial staff members regularly receive anonymous phone calls and letters.

Not all the protests came from expected sources. Bulk orders from churches were greatly reduced. Why? Perhaps one incident reported by a pastor is a clue. When a leading layman was asked at a board meeting to document his charge that the minister was too involved in radical activity, the best he could do was to exclaim, "Why, he had a stack of LIP's in his office!" The scene was repeated in other settings. A middle-class Negro leader complained that LIP was trying to make heroes out of black criminals, and a local college chaplain looked over the list of activist sponsors and decided that his counseling duties were too time-consuming to allow for his participation.

Obstacles were not all of this nay-saying variety. Some had to do with the ancient sin of acedia. A Pennsylvania Dutch community happy with its comfortable standard of living for the majority was simply too absorbed in its TV, gardening, and weekend at the shore to bother much about voice and concerns of the minority groups in their midst.

Circles of Support

We have spoken of the enthusiasm and dedication of the organizing core. In concentric rings around it are supporting orbits of persons who have contributed significantly to the life of LIP.

The first circle is made up of the hundreds of charter subscribers who saw the desperate need for representing the unrepresented news and views. Taking out subscriptions at $2 to $10 each were citizens of an adventurous bent and those associated with various movements for social justice. Among the first subscribers, although for different reasons, were community political leaders who watched the phenomenon with no little interest.

Among the churches that began with LIP and have been of special morale-boosting significance, one deserves special mention: the city's oldest and largest congregation, Trinity Lutheran Church. One of the first contacts the organizing group made in its brainstorming phase was with Dr. Wallace Fisher, the senior pastor and author of some well-known books on church renewal. Dr. Fisher gave the project his unreserved support. In addition to making available hundreds of copies of LIP on its literature table, the congregation runs regular ads and does an interpretive job with both the general public and some of the city's decision-makers. It is well to remember that when the newspaper takes a controversial stand on a local judge or a scattered-site housing program, it will be the participating churches and clergy whose locus is still within established Lancaster who feel the first shock waves. That is why there are not more Fishers and Trinitys. Fortunate is the community with its liberated churchmen.

Except for an occasional dissenter, the black community was enthusiastic in its reception of LIP, particularly black youths and young adults who had regularly received a bad press. While the rhetoric of black separatism is popular among these groups in Lancaster, as in most urban communities, a functional camaraderie below the level of ideology was born around the operation and services rendered by LIP. This has tended to bear out the hopes of the founders to find new areas of black-white cooperation based on the fact that each needs the other, to replace both the unities and disunities of old paternalisms and their backlash polarization.

Geographically on the farthest rim from the core are the out-of-town friends of LIP. Ranging from newspaper editors, church and secular—amazed to see the survival of the thing they forecast could never be born—through ACLU state officers, to Office of Economic Opportunity staff in Washington, planners in California, and Mennonite officials in Indiana, such counsel and support have been of great value. The largest delegation of extra-Lancaster support comes from United Church of Christ denominational leaders, agencies, and Conference executives.

As the sheer existence of LIP excites its antagonists, so its reality accounts for the interest and encouragement of its yea-sayers. It is proof that the voiceless can find their voice and claim their humanity.

Liberation Factors

What brought LIP to be in middle America and helped it to survive? Viewing it in two-year perspective, here are some crucial factors:

1. The momentum was built up by previous action in the community around such foci as Encounter (a downtown coffee-house renewal center), the Program for American Cultural Enrichment, efforts to eliminate de facto segregation in schools and housing and other civil-rights issues (see chapter 9). Out of this a loose coalition of people began to learn to work with each other. Also, their efforts were attended by some victories that convinced them that change could be effected.

2. The infusion of new blood into this mix contributes greatly, particularly high school students, young social workers, and black militants.

3. Related to the two above is what might be called the "McCarthy phenomenon." This is more than a spillover of the particular ex-McCarthyites. It is the emergence of a new, tough core of committed people in America who are willing to spend themselves for a humane society. Skeptical old-era politicians and other status quo types do not take into account this new readiness to "walk on water," and therefore they vastly miscalculate its potential.

4. The "Bull Connors effect" (named for the police chief of Birmingham, Alabama, in the sixties) is the presence and bum-

bling repressiveness of a monopoly media that invites and foments resistance to its actions and inactions.

5. The "Hatcher factor" is named for the black mayor of Gary, Indiana. As Mayor Hatcher is bolstered in many ways by foundations, educators, planners, and government sources, so LIP's future is tied up with its long-distance counsel and support. This is why some of the bitterest diatribes of the foes of social change are reserved for the "outside agitator."

6. Churchmen act as catalysts, community accreditors, and providers of some organizational and promotional savvy. In a pluralistic and secular society, church leaders cannot and should not attempt massive social change by themselves, for they are only a fraction of the community. But it is a layman, Saul Alinsky, who has discovered the clergymen who "burn with a white heat," and the civil-rights and peace movements that have learned to recognize kindred spirits among the renewal-oriented in the churches.

7. Issues of national import and momentum, the wave of concern about the need for a responsible media, and the appearance of both underground and independent presses around the country all contributed to the success of the local effort.

8. A headquarters serving both practical and symbolic functions was available; in this case, Encounter.

9. There has been avoidance of the adventurism and sensationalism in sex and revolutionary rhetoric which plays into the hands of those looking for ways to undermine a critical press.

10. Nonjournalistic, but nonetheless professional, skills of an array of volunteers are on tap: attorneys, advertising men, typists, photographers, writers, teachers, social workers.

11. A core of paid employees has evolved. As important as volunteers are, those who have worked in news forms of mission discover that summer vacations roll around, initial enthusiasms wear off, other challenges surface to compete. LIP's poorly paid editor is a decisive factor. The paper hopes to add a "real-life" reporter.

We spoke in our opening paragraph about the believable and the unbelievable. Can the latter survive the former? Will this fragile new growth bear up under the predictable pressures from those for whom the voice of the voiceless is an embarrassment and an offense? While no one is making firm predictions, new heart is taken each time the weekly miracle recurs. Its survival so far is indication that the tenacity of the Pennsylvania Dutchman, so long harnessed to horse-and-buggy commitments, can also be hitched to things of the future.

Two high school girls who write a youth column for LIP have named it "The Meek." We, too, believe that they shall inherit the earth.

Chapter 9
HUMANIZING
PUBLIC EDUCATION

Long before black studies were seen as a crucial educational tool for both understanding and identity, a small contingent of activists in America's hinterland were pioneering a program in black history and seeking to have its methodologies and content incorporated into the public-school system. Sensitive to the middle American character of Lancaster County, Pennsylvania, the architects of the project saw its possibility and promise in terms of a black-white constituency.

What Happened?

A dozen public-school teachers, black and white, gathered in the fall of 1964 at the initiative of the local theological seminary to examine what might be done to advance the human-rights struggle in their own sector. The teachers were deeply troubled about racial misinformation and voids in black culture in the public-school experience. Out of their dialogue came the determination to lift up for black children, and also for interested whites, the Afro-American heritage. The teachers also believed that the de facto segregation of the public schools contributed massively to white racism in the city, and denied quality education to both black and white students.

The first step in blackening education came in the spring of 1965 with the birth of PACE, the Program for American Cultural Enrichment. Launched by the teachers in cooperation with local civil-rights groups and churches, PACE was a seven-week Saturday course for a control group of thirty-two fifth- and sixth-graders, half of them black and half white. The program used the best available curriculum material produced by publishing houses alert to the freedom revolution, together with drama, music, crafts, and field trips to the site of the famous "Christiana riots" and stations on the underground of pre-Civil War days. Leadership came from nearby Philadelphia and the United Church of Christ Board for Homeland Ministries in the persons of black educators, Percel and May Alston, and the Board's staff member in residence at the seminary, Allen Kroehler, and his Laboratory for Leadership and Learning. PACE saw its role as demonstrating in miniature what the public-education Establishment could and should accomplish: integrated classes and teaching staff, training in effecting better human relationships, exposure to the facts about black history and culture that would both shatter white stereotypes and encourage a sense of self-worth in black children.

Participants and parents were so enthusiastic about their first year's experience that a second-year program was launched that enrolled 175 fifth-graders in eight classes held in church buildings around the city, and provided four adult courses on the freedom revolution and the issues of jobs, housing, and education. In an effort to give work to a black teacher displaced by southern desegregation, PACE developed a listing service for unemployed southern black teachers and obtained a full-time administrator for a three-month period from that source. It turned its data over to the school system with the hope that the administration would find the list useful when it needed personnel.

The following year PACE decided to concentrate its efforts in the ghetto schools and held another seven-week course for a group of eighty. By this time PACE had become a household word in the city and had received from the Community Council the coveted Community Betterment Award. But we are getting ahead of our story.

At the close of PACE's first year, one of the newspapers ran a sensational report on a critical study that PACE had made of the bias in a sixth grade social-studies text used by the school system. For several weeks articles and letters, many originating with the school administration, filled the pages of the paper with defenses of the textbook in question. Some attacked PACE and the seminary for "meddling." Although PACE was not particularly geared for controversy and many of its workers tended by nature to shy away from such furor, it nevertheless stood its ground and in fact mounted a stronger attack on the defects of the system. It became clearer from this confrontation that there was more to be done than lifting visions and developing educational models on the margin of community life. The public-school system itself had to be addressed.

The following fall (1965) a PACE political action committee was formed. The group sought out the services of Alexander Harper, newly appointed secretary for urban integration on the staff of the United Church of Christ Council for Christian Social Action, as consultant. Harper's first advice was to form a broad-based community task force that would address itself to the structural issues of public education. So ECC—the Educational Concerns Committee—came into existence, with representation from a wide spectrum of civil-rights, church, and other community groups. Claude Kilgore, a black clergyman who had just been called by the local Council of Churches as a metropolitan missioner with special responsibility in the ghetto, emerged as the natural leader of this task force.

After much debate, ECC focused on the integration of the three city junior high schools, with concomitant stress on textbook overhaul, black teacher recruitment and placement, and upgrading of "special education." A carefully researched document on the need for racial balance in the city schools, together with a map of how it could be attained at the junior high level, was drawn up by ECC members from Franklin and Marshall College in cooperation with Harper. ECC decided to channel the proposal through the education committee of the city-county Human Relations Committee in the hope that support from this quarter would strengthen its presentation to the school board. After heated debates this committee, whose membership included some school officials, adopted a slightly modified version of the original ECC document. This version called for commitment to an integrated school system and immediate implementation, but it did not formally endorse ECC's specific plan of redistricting the junior high schools.

The issue was now before the school board and being actively debated in the press. Out of the discussion finally came a timid and ambiguous acknowledgment by the board that there might be a problem and that perhaps it should be looked into. However mild this response, it was just enough to indicate an opening for change.

In the succeeding months ECC mustered its forces, appearing in strength at each board meeting. It kept up a steady drumbeat of public encouragement as well as protest about the delay in integrating the schools. Civil-rights and church groups gave support by a letter-writing campaign to the newspapers and by consultation with school-board members. The first hint of real progress came in the spring of 1966, when, on recommendation of the administration, the board voted a major expenditure for the purchase of multiethnic textbooks in a variety of subjects and for new social-studies textbooks revised by publishers in the wake of the freedom revolution. The textbook earlier in dispute was quietly dropped. On the heels of this, the board went on to propose—with several vocal dissents—launching "a modified open enrollment plan," granting voluntary pupil movement anywhere in the city, on the condition that it benefited racial balance in the elementary and junior high schools.

The fall saw a tiny delegation of sixteen students (twelve black and four white) apply for transfer under the open enrollment plan. ECC had resisted the plan, although it had succeeded in modifying it so that pupil transfer was permitted only for reasons of racial balance. But now ECC openly criticized the program as placing the financial and psychological burdens for restructuring the schools upon ghetto parents. The program really boiled down to abdication of responsibility by the administration and board. ECC again began mass public appearances and testimony at board meetings.

In December 1966 a picture appeared in one of the papers showing the school superintendent poised over a city map with a handful of pins ready for placement. Accompanying it was the announcement of an administration plan to redistrict the junior high schools.

In the opening months of 1967 things got lively on "Cabbage Hill," a Caucasian blue-collar district adjacent to the Seventh Ward whose junior high would be receiving black pupils, and part of whose youth would be transferred into the Seventh Ward junior high. A group calling themselves PET (Parents, Educators, and Taxpayers), formed during the early PACE days but so far ineffectual, suddenly took on menacing proportions. It managed to collect a thousand signatures opposing redistricting; it recruited hundreds for a protest meeting; and it sent a barrage of letters to the editor of one of the newspapers. One paper spoke gravely about the evils of the innovation. Another daily, which had given extensive and fair coverage to PACE-ECC affairs, came out for redistricting. Also endorsing the move with enthusiasm were the Education Committee of the Human Relations Committee, local chapters of the NAACP and of the Urban League (the Congress of Racial Equality and the Student Nonviolent Coordinating Committee have no organizations in Lancaster), and community groups ranging from the Social Action Committee (Council of Churches) to the Great Books Club.

At a stormy school-board meeting in February 1967, held in a downtown auditorium to accommodate the crowd, members voted 6 to 3 to redistrict the schools according to the administration proposal, which involved the redistribution of pupils over a three-year period. Although the staggered time schedule modified ECC's original plan, the move was on the whole a striking advance in imagination and action for a conservative Pennsylvania Dutch city. Several months later a modest realignment of elementary school districts was quietly accomplished, on the grounds that a newly constructed school in the area necessitated pupil reshuffling. This rationale was offered by administration officials in addition to the need for racial balance for the junior high redistricting.

Noting the importance of political factors in the school drive, ECC, together with NAACP, turned its attention next to the election of responsible school leadership. This new interest in politics got a cool reception from both political parties, and the petition to nominate black candidates was turned aside with the advice that "the time was not yet ripe." Angered by this paternalism, ECC and NAACP members (the latter organization could not formally endorse candidates) ran a black write-in candidate, Lionel Cunningham, on the Democratic ballot in the spring primaries, much to the distress of the party machine, which was fearful of the retribution of Cabbage Hill constituency. With a vigorous new sense of identity won by taking on a Goliath, ghetto residents canvassed the inner city, and set up and executed an ambitious election day get-out-the-vote drive for their candidate. By ECC tabulation, the write-in candidate got over half the votes garnered by regular party candidates (although the official tally fixed the number at about the quarter mark, because of invalidation of numerous stickers that never found their exact location in the obscure writing slot of the voting machine). But even though their candidate lost, the black community had found its voice.

In the succeeding months the ECC write-in candidate was appointed by the mayor to the Redevelopment Authority and now serves as its secretary. In 1969 the Democratic party ran Mr. Cunningham for the school board on its official slate. He lost in the Republican landslide of that year, but another battle had been won. Another PACE-ECC black leader, a woman, was the first of her sex (but not of her race) to join the Housing Authority.

The struggle is, of course, not all over. PET, now under the wing of the new rightist Constitution party, has run candidates for school board (though with small showings). There remains the possibility that an increasingly right-wing board might someday reverse the 1967 decision. But each year that prospect becomes less likely, for the junior high schools are now fully integrated and The End has not come. Even the local daily that objected so strenuously to the desegregation has surveyed the results and pronounced its reluctant blessing. The fears of white parents that black children will demoralize "their" schools have virtually disappeared. The superintendent himself has announced that all "is going very well." In fact, educators around the state make regular inquiries of the school staff to find out what the secret of such a progressive administration might be.

How Come?

What indeed are the "secrets?" There are none, but it is possible to pinpoint factors that made community change smoother.

1. Dedicated core. The catalytic agent in the change process appeared to be the core of committed people willing to see the program through to fruition. This kind of persistence and perseverance entailed "focus." It meant that other needs would have gone begging if they had depended for their basic support on this particular cadre of the concerned. This suggests an adaptation of the concept of "orders" to the social mission of the church. Rather than expecting everyone to do everything, it seems to make more sense to train teams of those ready for mission, each having its "portfolio" in one (or more than one) critical human issue, to whom others look as their tutors and representatives on that frontier. These same others, of course, must make themselves available to participate in that venture when they are needed.

2. The broad base of the team. The representative character of the Lancaster task force meant that it had lines open to a variety of people and groups in the city. Church people by themselves cannot hope to effect significant social change in a pluralistic situation. The seed group was cross-cultural, interracial, bipartisan, interfaith.

3. Situational focus. While the local effort reflected issues national in scope, neither abstract theories nor ideology controlled the choice of concerns or the way they were addressed. The immediate needs of a particular eastern Pennsylvania community were kept in the foreground, and the methods used to meet those needs arose out of the particular ethos of that community.

4. The "outside agitator." Though he is a favorite scapegoat of bigots, North and South, the roving reformer is a crucial person in community change. Staff members of national Christian-education and social-action organizations were important sources of help to PACE and ECC. The timely coming of the national NAACP in the person of the district director (and references to the local problem in speeches by visiting Urban League dignitaries, including the national education director Frank Stanley, Jr., and Whitney Young himself) gave hefty accreditation to local efforts. The national ferment of the freedom revolution that the visitors represented gave an air of familiarity to the issues fought out at home, so that the community was not totally unprepared for innovations sought by PACE and ECC.

5. Establishment allies. Not all the committed can or ought to be at the barricades in some—perhaps in most—such efforts. There are those in a position to make decisions or influence those who do. These people can play a crucial role as agents of change. A ranking conservative of one political party, who was on the school board, as well as the president of the seminary, did yeoman work at key moments. The editor of one of the city's newspapers, Redevelopment Authority staff members, people in social-action organizations, courageous local clergy speaking the right word at the right time, local churches offering space in their buildings for PACE and other projects, lay organizations performing important shirt-sleeve tasks ranging from PACE canvassing to ECC-sponsored attendance at school-board meetings—all played vital parts.

6. The emergence of black presence and power. Although the

110

spawning ground of PACE was a mixed teachers' group, the program underscored black self-esteem. Philadelphia resource personnel at the beginning, and soon thereafter the southern administrator, and the local lay leadership were from the black community. Building on this momentum in PACE, ECC began with black leadership, basically middle class in character, but soon developed strong grass-roots support and leadership in the ghetto paralleling a similar development in PACE. The weaving of its life into the day-to-day Seventh Ward fabric of drugstores, taverns, street corners, fraternal and church groups, and its door-to-door contact methods established ECC's drive for integration as a natural part of the life of the area. The support given to the write-in candidate on short notice with no resources served notice to the party machinery that there was a new voice and spirit to be reckoned with in a part of town long considered powerless or manipulable.

7. The resource role of whites. Throughout the three-year struggle, whites saw their function as supportive and secondary. It came in the form of research through the academic channels of Franklin and Marshall College and Lancaster Theological Seminary, through interpretation to the white community and recruitment from it, and through general availability when needed and sought after by black leadership. In the context of a small city with 6 percent black citizenry and 10 percent black school population, pragmatists both black and white were little attracted to the anticoalition ideologies generated in large urban centers. But the motif of leadership by the black of his own revolution was very much part of the Lancaster effort, from its beginnings in the PACE training in black identity to its current struggle for black political power.

8. A symbolic "headquarters." PACE, ECC, and its allies tended to gravitate to Encounter, a church-sponsored coffeehouse and renewal center. Here were held PACE exhibits on Negro art and history, ECC and PACE planning meetings, community forums on de facto segregation and textbook bias, and the original sessions initiated by the seminary students that set forth some of the movement's leading themes. In a later phase, Encounter became the location of "Freedom House," a NAACP-sponsored youth headquarters and program that made the center a natural gathering place for many in the Seventh Ward who came to

111

take part in PACE-ECC thrusts. The liveliest use of Encounter came on primary election day in 1967, when the building served as nerve center of the write-in campaign, complete with the litter of handbills, coffee for the milling precinct workers, and radio election returns.

9. The media. By both accident and design, PACE and ECC had an interested and active press. The novelty of PACE in the Pennsylvania Dutch hinterlands made good copy for the three newspapers in the city. Controversy, editorials, and a boiling letters-to-the-editor column gave the issues wide and constant exposure. And the more acrimony there was in the attacks of the conservative press and the PET group, the more esprit and solidarity developed in the ghetto.

10. A think-tank. Collection and interpretation of data and reflection on the direction and meaning of the struggle were tasks done by area academic communities, including faculty and students at Franklin and Marshall and Millersville Colleges, but principally Lancaster Theological Seminary. Although the seminary had no official connection with the movement (some of its sharpest critics were the few students who "were sick and tired of hearing about PACE and ECC"), students in Christian Ethics courses—which were predicated on "reflection in the context of involvement"—took an active part in many of the phases, as did student wives, who helped to initiate PACE and continued to work in it and the community confrontations on redistricting. The seminary's Laboratory for Leadership and Learning housed the PACE resources and later the PACE administrator. Some faculty members and faculty wives gave unstintingly of their time, and the faculty as a whole performed an accrediting role on occasion with a public statement. The part that the seminary president played on the school board was noted earlier.

11. Relation of core group to other rights groups. Conceived from the beginning as ad hoc in nature, with heavy representation from other elements in the civil-rights movement, PACE and ECC sustained cordial relations with their allies. Support came at crucial moments from both local chapters and national staff of NAACP and the Urban League. The education subcommittee of the city-county Human Relations Committee proved throughout to be a valuable sounding board and liaison agent on the outer rim of Establishment Lancaster.

What Does It Mean?

Two general observations may be made:

Steps toward the elimination of de facto segregation, at the present so beset by difficulties in the large urban centers, may be within reach of smaller urban communities.

Coalition efforts are both a possibility and a necessity in this kind of context.

More specifically, the whole effort and experience teaches much about church strategy for social mission. Here are some lessons:

1. The church can make a difference in the struggle to humanize the structures of public education. In the Lancaster situation the work of laity and clergy ranged from approving the use of buildings for PACE activities and grinding the mimeograph and visiting PACE parents to church auxiliaries that showed up en masse at critical school-board meetings and stands taken by preachers and council at the height of controversy. Further, there was the use of Encounter as headquarters and the activities of national church staff members and the Council of Churches' missionary.

2. Rigid institutional patterns are not changed by exhortation and moral suasion, but by the responsible use of social power. The massing of ghetto sentiment, the public demonstration, the vocal stands of community groups and leaders, the power of the news media, and the vote were important factors. (It should be noted, however, that there were some impressive exceptions, in which grasp of the facts and a sensitive conscience appeared to be at work.) The Christian view of sin, its depth and persistence, was borne out in this confrontation.

3. The massive hurts of the city, and the healing possible through effective action, should make the serving of human needs one of the mission priorities of the church in urban society. On Jericho roads, Samaritans first bind up wounds. The mission of the church is not exhausted in ministry to the neighbor, of course; but its calling to tell and celebrate the Christian story must always be fulfilled in the midst of human ferment.

4. Mission is carried out in a pioneering-relinquishing style. Thus the church is called to lift up a vision of healing (PACE as a tiny model of reconciliation and educational excellence in

the race issue), then to try to stir the larger community to its own proper responsibility (ECC's prodding function), and then to fold its own institutional tents to move on to the next unseen and unmet need when the human community as a whole accepts its responsibilities (PACE's hope that it can work itself out of a job).

5. The church is called to address the corporate structures of the city, in this case the public-school system and the political machinery. Its claim arises from the simple mandate of a neighbor love that seeks to use the most effective means at hand to heal human hurt. The New Testament recognition of the Lordship of Christ over the principalities and powers is further confirmation of this ministry. The pluriform nature of church mission means that decisions have to be made about what structures are viable.

6. Theology comes alive in the heat of mission. Laity and clergy, students and faculty grew in their understanding of the biblical themes of the work of Christ in the world, the nature of sin, the principalities and powers, and the eschatological signs of hope in history. And the quality of worship and the meaning of faith itself were not left untouched. The Teacher is found in his classroom in the world.

7. Churchmen must be prepared to pay the cost of sharp community conflict: economic reprisal, acrimonious attack in the press, threats of violence and their occasional implementation, the anonymous phone call and letter, jeopardy to the institutions to which one is attached, the cold shoulder in established circles, both church and secular. These, however, are small irritants compared to the larger sacrifices faithful men are called to make on other terrain.

Shortly after the school-board vote on redistricting, Encounter sported a new graffiti wall, inviting philosophical scribble from its visitors. It was christened by an NAACP militant with a large-lettered "HOPE?"

Sober hope, that is the idiom of faith. Along with a future-oriented generation, it looks forward to the shape of things to come. Aware as it is of the frailty of every human advance, it nevertheless believes with Martin Luther King, Jr., that men have a right to dream. And it points to, and works within, the historical harbingers of a better world that beckons from out ahead. Those who have taken part in the birth pangs of something important to the people of a small city believe they have seen such a portent.

Chapter 10

THE LIBERATED MIDDLE

An uncorseted midsection? A town square taken from the enemy? No, nothing so dramatic. "Mid-libs" are those among the country's silent center who have been "freed up."

Art Buchwald calls them the "radical middle," that space of "moderate madness . . . [that] lies between Spiro and Abbie."[1] Mad, yes. Radical, no. Radicals, like reactionaries, are captives. They are imprisoned in predesigned response patterns. What is more predictable than an Establishment newspaper editorial on pot? An underground newspaper editorial on pot.

There is a new breed aborning. Not much notice has been taken of it because of our category foul-up. We slip the liberated ones under our careless labels of polarity. When we see those long graying sideburns swinging along in a peace demonstration, we know it is just another left-winger. Or that Sierra Club matron leading the campaign to send back the six-packs is really on a derring-do fling, and may even be out to divert the Movement. No, sir. These are the "mid-libs" that do not fit into the molds contrived by the ideologues. They have been conditioned by the ethos of middle America, but not programmed. They are free to be.

In the grand tradition of humanism, influenced too by our pragmatic temper, the mid-lib has broken out of his ideological prisons. He calls them as he sees them. Here is an open wound. There is a festering sore. The Samaritan leaps to heal the hurt. He has shaken loose from complex blueprints and simple slogans that prescribe what must be done and where.

While liberated from system-slavery, action is not helter-skelter. The mid-lib has a framework, or, more accurately, a vision. He wants a world that is, like him, free to be. And more, free to be together. "Free to be" is liberation. "Together" is shalom, a world at one with itself. This kind of healing covers all the wounds of nature and man. It is the dream of a time when wolf and lamb will lie down together, when swords will be beaten into ploughshares, where each person lives at peace within and without under vine and fig tree. That vision draws him into all the struggles of participatory shalom—the liberation of black, poor, young, unblack, unpoor, unyoung, women, the movements for peace among nations and persons, and for ecological harmony between man and nature.

The mid-lib is risk oriented and characterized by a low boiling point. He acts while others speculate or temporize. The risk of the act is its potential cost—at the least, being counted the fool; at the most, loss of livelihood and sometimes limb and life.

But the mid-lib is not usually a heroic figure fresh from Sherwood Forest. He often just stumbles into controversy and backs into the barricades. Middle-aged middle-libs may be hurled into the arena because their young are under attack. And their children, themselves neophyte mid-libs, may have been prodded awake simply because of their proximity and vulnerability to the action. Witness Cambodia, Kent State, and their aftermath. Invariably, self-interest is somehow tangled up with overcoming the oppression of others.

Indeed, there are more mid-libs than the reactionaries or the revolutionaries care to admit. And they pack more of a wallop than their numbers would indicate. The exploited have launched their own freedom movements; black power, poor power, student power, and woman power are basic to liberation. But mid-libs are the swing factor in these struggles and the key to the freedom struggle of middle America itself.

Because of their potential power, sharp-eyed change agents court mid-libs. Revolutionaries and reactionaries flirt with them, too, but finally reject them for their independence. And the yet-to-be-liberated silent center from which they spring often fume at their treason. Liberation breeds homelessness.

Acts of Mid-Liberation

Here is a high school junior wearing a black armband on Moratorium Day. She is suspended by an administrator long accustomed to unchallenged control over the lives of students. Not this time. The girl and twenty peers picket the principal. Two blue-collar middle American parents, also distressed about the war and awakened to the dangers of repression, employ an attorney. The lawyer is one of four in the local profession who dare to take civil-rights cases, in spite of sanctions by their fraternity.

117

The next day this cadre of mid-libs gains two teachers, who risk the derision of their colleagues and possible loss of jobs by donning their own black armbands.

The developers are coming. Fat cats with their mainland money are buying up Hawaiian shorelines long held in trust for native Polynesians. How the hotel and condominium builders would like to get that valley just outside suburban Honolulu for the retired rich and the tourist trade! But lined up against the technocratic club of developers-land trustees-big industry-government is an odd assortment: ordinary suburbanites near whose homes a proposed freeway will pour its tourist hotels and affluent new residents, an army of surfing buffs whose beaches and waters will be destroyed by mountain-moving tractors and sluices of fresh sewage from the developments, ecology crusaders now prepared for their last stand against the destroyers of an already-dying Pacific paradise, and the native Hawaiians themselves who live in the valley as pig farmers or as working-class homeowners. This strange coalition petitions, pickets, and sits in at the statehouse. It will probably lose this one but not the next one, for the freed-up ranks of mid-Pacific middle Americans are swelling.

The city has had its share of demonstrations in the sixties, led by a corporal's guard of civil-rights and peace activists. Yet now, on the doorstep of a new decade, the main street is ablaze with the light of a half-mile long procession of candles. Silent as the deaths they are mourning, they occupy center city. The college young are in the lead, but with them are the squarest of citizens, from merchants and mailmen to engineers, nurses, and Vietnam veterans. The horror of gunfire on the campuses and in the rice paddies is remembered and repudiated by a growing company of those sprung loose from the sidelines.

"I hear about riots, war, and protest all week. When I go to church on Sunday I want peace." Here and there are clergy who refuse the cry for cheap peace. They incur the wrath of their congregation's power structure, and not infrequently are asked to leave because they defend the stand of a National Council of Churches or Vatican II on the rights of the poor, selective conscientious objection, racial justice. Some go from strength to strength because they serve churches that have moved from polarization through self-purgation to a reduced, but cleansed, community supporting the freedom of the pulpit and its relevance. The mid-libs leave their mark alongside the cross and the Star of David.

For years spinach looked like spinach to Mrs. Zavodnick. But now she found herself scrubbing a bunch three times before cooking it. And even then the discolored water in the pan told her she had not won the battle with the new pesticides. After complaining to the supermarket manager and wondering out loud why they still stocked so many products laced with poisonous additives and never had any "health foods," she was passed off as one of those crackpots. But when Mrs. Zavodnick organized an informal boycott among the neighbors, the offending items began to disappear, strange new labels elbowed their way onto the shelves, and even the front window sported a display from the local Good Earth chapter. After she became one of the 700,000 subscribers to the formerly obscure organic gardening magazine coming out of Emmaus, Pennsylvania, no food moguls were going to put anything over on her. Further, while mill-town families have always liked having gardens, the Zavodnick back yard was now becoming an important source of nourishment (and disposal), with its organic crops and compost piles. On top of these changing habits, Mrs. Zavodnick—no fan of "protestors"—found herself one sunny Earth Day out in the street with the flower children listening to a speech by one of Nader's raiders and passing out petitions to get the Food and Drug Administration to do its business.

Life-styles can change. They do, and will.

The Future of Mid-Liberation

Like the silent womb from which they came, the liberated middle is not organized. As groupy as any Americans, they have a thirst for belonging but are mobile in their associations. One finds them linked up with this, that, or the other movement of liberative shalom.

Has the time come for mid-libs to find their soul brothers? Is it the moment for marshaling the troops of liberation? Probably not. The special gift of the mid-libs is the grace with which they move among the current ideologies and their institutions without captivity to any Babylon. They organize ad hoc, not per se.

But they need to know who they are. That self-consciousness will sustain them in their invisible community as surely as the ancient believer was nourished by his communion of saints.

For what can they hope? At first, here a victory, there a victory, liberated zones that promise growth as the middle American consciousness is raised. To stretch the boundaries of these colonies is the task of the seventies. And the goal of the decade: to edge liberation in middle America toward liberation of middle America.

NOTES

PREFACE

1. Gabriel Fackre, *The Promise of Reinhold Niebuhr* (New York: Lippincott, 1970).

Chapter 1
THE BLUE-GREENING OF AMERICA

1. Louise Kapp Howe, ed., *The White Majority* (New York: Random House, 1970), p. 295. Other journalist inquiries cited in this paragraph are Peter Binzen, *Whitetown, USA* (New York: Random House, 1970); Richard Lemon, *The Troubled American* (New York: Simon and Schuster, 1970); Marshall Frady, "Gary, Indiana," *Harper's Magazine* (August 1969) and idem, *Wallace* (New York: Meridian Books, World Publishing, 1971); Studs Terkel, *Hard Times* (New York: Random House, 1970); Richard Scammon and Ben Wattenberg, *The Real Majority* (New York: Coward-McCann, 1970). See also "Man and Woman of the Year: The Middle Americans," *Time* (January 5, 1970), pp. 10-17; "The Blue Collar Worker's Lowdown Blues," *Time* (November 9, 1970); "A Rising Cry: 'Ethnic Power,'" *Newsweek* (December 21, 1970), pp. 33-36.

2. Frank Armbruster, "Misunderstood Americans and U.S. Policy," mimeographed (New York: Hudson Research Institute, 1970). Other references are Andrew Greeley, *Why Can't They Be Like Us?* (New York: E. P. Dutton & Co., 1971); Arthur Shostak, *Blue-Collar Life* (New York: Random House, 1969); Joseph Bensman and Arthur Vidich, *The New American Society: The Revolution of the Middle Class* (Chicago: *Quadrangle Books,* 1971), Judith Magidson, *The Reacting Americans* (New York: The American Jewish Committee, 1968); Nathan Glazer and Daniel Moynihan, *Beyond the Melting Pot* (Cambridge, Mass.: M.I.T. Press,

1963) ; Mirra Komarovsky, *Blue-Collar Marriage* (New York: Random House, 1962) ; C. Wright Mills, *White Collar* (New York: Oxford University Press, 1951). For a fascinating photographic essay see Robert Coles and Jon Erikson, *The Middle Americans* (Boston: Little, Brown and Company, 1971).

3. Sam Brown, "The Same Old Gang Turns Up in Washington," *Life*, 70, no. 3 (January 29, 1971) : 2.

4. Saul Alinsky, *Rules for Radicals* (New York: Random House, 1971), p. 185. See also Marion K. Sanders, *The Professional Radical: Conversation with Saul Alinsky* (New York: Harper & Row, 1970), pp. 67-93.

5. Hannah Arendt, *On Violence* (New York: Harcourt, Brace, & World, 1970), passim.

6. Scammon and Wattenberg, *The Real Majority*, pp. 46-81. For a powerful interpretation of the world's "real majority," see Colin Morris, *Unyoung, Uncolored, Unpoor* (Nashville: Abingdon Press, 1969).

7. In general agreement with the location of our range are Lemon's sampling in *The Troubled American,* p. 7; Michael Schneider in his helpful essay "Middle America: Study in Frustration," *Center Magazine,* 3, no. 6 (November/December 1970) : 2; Alinsky, quoted in Sanders, *The Professional Radical,* p. 68; and Scammon and Wattenberg, *The Real Majority,* p. 54

8. W. Lloyd Warner with Martha Meeker and Kenneth Wells, *Social Class in America* (New York: Harper & Row, 1960), passim.

9. Mills, *White Collar*, pp. 63-76; Bensman and Vidich, *The New American Society,* pp. 5-6.

10. On mill-town issues, *The Purpose and Work of the Ministry* (Philadelphia: Christian Education Press, 1959), and on modern alienation, "A Comparison and Critique of the Interpretation of Dehumanization in the Thought of Sören Kierkegaard and Karl Marx" (doctoral diss., University of Chicago, 1962).

11. Peter Berger and Brigitte Berger, "The Blueing of America," *New Republic,* 164, no. 20 (April 3, 1971) : 21-23.

12. John Orr and F. Patrick Nelson, *The Radical Suburb* (Philadelphia: Westminster Press, 1970).

Chapter 2
DEHUMANIZATION IN MIDDLE AMERICA

1. We deal in this typology with the kind of dehumanization critique that located the source of the problem in an image and structural relationship emanating from an "other." There was another form of depersonalization analysis, fathered by Kierkegaard, which found the self to be the root of alienation. See Gabriel Fackre, "A Comparison and Critique of the Interpretation of Dehumanization in the Thought of Sören Kierkegaard and Karl Marx" (doctoral diss., University of Chicago, 1962), pp. 8-101, 268-82.
2. Erich Fromm, *The Sane Society* (New York: Rinehart, 1955), pp. 93, 95, 139.
3. Paul Tillich, *The Protestant Era* (Chicago: University of Chicago Press, 1948), p. 255.
4. Helmut Gollwitzer, *Unwilling Journey* (Philadelphia: Muhlenberg Press, 1953), pp. 40-44.
5. Helmut Thielicke, *Nihilism* (New York: Harper, 1961), pp. 32-34.
6. Arthur Koestler, *Darkness at Noon* (New York: Macmillan, 1941), pp. 157-161.
7. C. Wright Mills, *White Collar* (New York: Oxford University Press, 1951), pp. 182-88.
8. Harvey Cox, *The Secular City* (New York: Macmillan, 1965), pp. 199-204 (first appeared as "Playboy's Doctrine of the Male," *Christianity and Crisis*, 21, no. 6 (April 17, 1961).
9. Fromm, *The Sane Society*, pp. 110-20.
10. Roland Berg, "A Report on Hospitals," *Look*, 23, no. 3 (February 3, 1959): 15-19.
11. Martin Buber, *I and Thou* (Edinburgh: T & T Clark, 1937), pp. 16 ff.
12. Martin Buber, *Paths in Utopia* (New York: Macmillan, 1949).
13. Fromm, *The Sane Society*, pp. 303-31.
14. Editors of *Fortune, The Exploding Metropolis* (New York: Doubleday, 1958).
15. Lewis Mumford, *In the Name of Sanity* (New York: Harcourt, Brace, & World, 1954), pp. 224-33; Robert Nisbet, *The*

Quest for Community (New York: Oxford University Press, 1953), pp. 274-79.

16. See editorial in *The Christian Century*, 75, no. 6 (February 11, 1959): 156-57.

17. Will Herberg, ed., Introduction to *The Writings of Martin Buber* (New York: Meridian, 1956), p. 22.

18. Michael Harrington, *The Other America* (Baltimore: Penguin Books, 1963).

19. Bernard Rosenberg and David White, eds., *Mass Culture* (New York: Free Press of Glencoe, 1957); and Eric Larrabee and Rolf Meyersohn, *Mass Leisure* (New York: Free Press of Glencoe, 1958).

20. Vance Packard, *The Hidden Persuaders* (New York: David McKay Co., 1957).

21. Joost Meerloo, *The Rape of the Mind* (Cleveland: World, 1956).

22. Rosenberg and White, *Mass Culture*, pp. 3-12.

23. Herbert Marcuse, *Reason and Revolution* (Boston: Beacon Press, 1960), pp. 273-87.

24. Fromm, *The Sane Society*, pp. 120-90.

25. C. Golden and H. Rutenburg, *Dynamics of Industrial Democracy* (New York: Harper, 1942), pp. 7, 8, 183.

26. *Mater et Magistra*, quoted in *Light*, 6, no. 8 (August 1961): 5.

27. Elton Mayo, *The Human Problems of an Industrial Civilization* (Cambridge, Mass.: Harvard Business School, 1946).

28. Sidney Lens, *The Crisis of American Labor* (New York: Sagamore, 1959), pp. 226-51.

29. Martin Luther King, Jr., *Stride toward Freedom* (New York: Harper, 1958).

30. "The Port Huron Statement" (1962), in Paul Jacobs and Saul Landau, *The New Radicals* (Middlesex, England: Penguin, 1966), pp. 154-67.

31. Theodore Roszak, *The Making of a Counter Culture* (New York: Anchor Books, Doubleday, 1969).

32. Alvin Toffler, *Future Shock* (New York: Random House, 1970).

33. Alexander Campbell, *The Trouble with Americans* (New York: Praeger, 1971), passim.

34. "The Special All-Amerikan Issue," *Argus*, 6, no. 3 (January

1971). This University of Maryland student publication, which purports to describe middle America, is a sample of the stereotyping which plays neatly into the hands of those who would like to keep the dehumanized busy with their civil war.

Chapter 3
BEING HUMAN IN MIDDLE AMERICA

1. See Gabriel Fackre, *Humiliation and Celebration: Post-Radical Themes in Doctrine, Morals, and Mission* (New York: Sheed & Ward, 1969).

Chapter 4
WORK AND PLAY IN MILL TOWN

1. Arnold Hutschnecker, *Will to Live*, rev. ed. (Englewood Cliffs, N.J.: Prentice-Hall, 1958), p. 49.

Chapter 5
THE BLUE-COLLAR WHITE AND THE FAR RIGHT

1. Quoted in Marshall Frady, *Wallace* (New York: Meridian Books, World Publishing Company, 1968), pp. 14, 20, 25.
2. Ibid., pp. 27-28.

Chapter 7
AQUARIAN DREAMS AND EARTHED HOPES

1. See Gabriel Fackre, *Humiliation and Celebration: Post-Radical Themes in Doctrine, Morals, and Mission* (New York: Sheed & Ward, 1969), chapters 5-8; and Gabriel Fackre, *The Rainbow Sign* (Grand Rapids: W. D. Eerdmans Company, 1969), pp. 45-69.

Chapter 10
THE LIBERATED MIDDLE

1. Art Buchwald, "The Radical Middle," *The Washington Post*, May 3, 1970, p. b 7. See also Renata Adler, *Toward a Radical Middle* (New York: Random House, 1969), especially pp. xiii-xxiv.